THE CHILDREN'S TREASURY OF
CLASSIC
POETRY

THE COMPILER

Nicola Baxter has written or compiled over two hundred children's titles. She has developed ideas for a wide variety of international publishers and particularly enjoys the marriage of words and pictures that children's books entail. She lives in Norfolk, England, with her little daughter.

THE ILLUSTRATOR

Cathie Shuttleworth was trained in calligraphy, heraldry and illumination. Through her work with the Royal College of Arms, she has produced coats of arms for the wedding of HRH Prince Andrew and other royal projects, but her real love is illustration, particularly of a wide range ofchildren's books. She lives in a village in Northamptonshire, England.

THE CHILDREN'S TREASURY OF
CLASSIC
POETRY

Compiled by
NICOLA BAXTER

Illustrated by
CATHIE SHUTTLEWORTH

BARNES
&NOBLE
BOOKS
NEW YORK

This edition published by Barnes & Noble, Inc.,
by arrangement with Bookmart.

2000 Barnes & Noble Books

First published in 2000 by Armadillo Books
An imprint of Bookmart Limited
Desford Road, Enderby
Leicester LE9 5AD
England

© 2000 Bookmart Limited

Originally published by Bookmart Limited as
The Children's Classic Poetry Collection
and *Classic Poetry for Children*

M 10 9 8 7 6 5 4 3 2 1

ISBN 0-7607-2266-8

Produced by Nicola Baxter
Designed by Amanda Hawkes

Printed in Italy

CONTENTS

ANIMALS AND BIRDS

The Owl and the Pussy-Cat	12
Jabberwocky	14
Hurt No Living Thing	16
Auguries of Innocence	16
How Doth the Little Crocodile	18
The Herring Loves the Merry Moonlight	19
The Maldive Shark	19
My Cat Jeoffry	20
The Owl	22
The Silver Swan	23
The Eagle	23
The Tyger	24

WEATHER AND SEASONS

Whether the Weather Be Fine	26
It's Raining, It's Pouring	26
The Rainbow	27
The Wind	28
The North Wind Doth Blow	28
Windy Nights	29

The Human Seasons	30
Winter	32
Spring	33
From Rain in Summer	34
Fall, Leaves, Fall	35
The Year's at the Spring	36

BRIGHT AND BEAUTIFUL

Pied Beauty	38
Daffodils	39
My Shadow	40
The Ecchoing Green	42
She Walks in Beauty	44
Shall I Compare Thee to a Summer's Day?	45
Blow, Bugle, Blow	46

CONTENTS

DREAMS AND WONDERS

Kubla Khan   48
The Fairies   50
La Belle Dame Sans Mercie   52
I Saw a Peacock   54
A Child's Thought   54

SONGS OF THE SEA

Full Fathom Five   56
What Are Heavy   57
I Started Early   58
O Captain! My Captain!   60
Break, Break, Break   62
Meeting at Night   64

TALES OF TRAVEL

Ozymandias   66
Where Lies the Land   67
Eldorado   68
Foreign Lands   70
Uphill   71
Travel   72
From a Railway Carriage   74

CHILDHOOD

Little Orphant Annie   76
Monday's Child   78
A Child's Grace   79
I Remember, I Remember   80
Swing, Swing   82
Good and Bad Children   84

AT THE END OF THE DAY

Escape at Bedtime   86
Bed in Summer   88
Is the Moon Tired?   89
Wynken, Blynken, and Nod   90
Star Light, Star Bright   92
How Many Miles to Babylon   92
Hush Little Baby   93
Sleep, Baby, Sleep!   94

CONTENTS

LOVE AND ADVENTURE

Robin Hood	98
A Red, Red, Rose	100
A Birthday	101
Lochinvar	102
A New Courtly Sonnet of the Lady Greensleeves	104
The Night Has a Thousand Eyes	106

SONGS AND BALLADS

Thomas the Rhymer	108
Bonny Barbara Allan	112
The Great Silkie of Sule Skerrie	114
The Yarn of the Nancy Bell	116

BOYS AND GIRLS

What Am I After All	122
Jemima	123
There was a Naughty Boy	124
The False Knight and the Wee Boy	126
Children	128
When That I Was and a Little Tiny Boy	130

MAGIC AND MYSTERY

Waltzing Matilda	132
The Ghost's Song	133
John Barleycorn	134
A Strange Visitor	137
The Oxen	140

CONTENTS

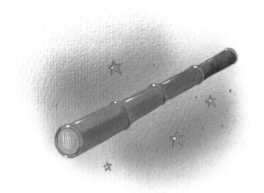

SIGHTS AND SOUNDS

Upon Westminster Bridge   142
On First Looking into
    Chapman's Homer   143
Symphony in Yellow   144
A Thing of Beauty   145
From the Garden   146

SADNESS AND HAPPINESS

So, We'll Go No More
    A-Roving   154
Spring and Fall   155
Canadian Boat Song   156
In the Highlands   158
When in Disgrace With
    Fortune   159
Piping Down the Valleys Wild   160
A Lark's Nest   161
From The Song of Solomon   161
The Swing   162
Requiem   163

MUSIC AND DANCING

Song's Eternity   148
Music   150
Piano   151
I Am of Ireland   152

About the Poets   165

Glossary   171

Index of Titles and First Lines 173

INTRODUCTION

In this collection of well-loved poems, you will see amazing sights, meet strange and spooky people and read words that may make you sing, dance and even cry.

Poets use words in a special way. They seem to be able to squeeze lots of meanings and feelings into just a few lines. Sometimes it is hard to understand everything the poet is saying. That may be because a poem was written long ago or uses a kind of English that is unlike the language you speak. Don't worry if you can't understand everything. Poems can surprise and please you each time you read them, as you understand a little more each time.

It is always a good idea to try reading a poem aloud. Some odd words make sense as soon as you say them. And even if parts of the poem sound strange and mysterious, you will be able to hear the rhythm and rhyme of the lines, which is just what the poet wanted you to do.

At the end of the book, you will find a glossary of the most difficult words of all—the ones I had to look up in a dictionary, too! There is also some information about the poets and an index of titles and first lines, so it will always be easy for you to find the poems you like best and read them over and over again!

N.M.A.B.

ANIMALS
and
BIRDS

The Owl and the Pussy-Cat

The Owl and the Pussy-Cat went to sea
In a beautiful pea-green boat,
They took some honey, and plenty of money;
Wrapped up in a five-pound note.
The Owl looked up to the stars above,
And sang to a small guitar,
"O lovely Pussy, O Pussy, my love,
What a beautiful Pussy you are,
　　You are,
　　You are!
What a beautiful Pussy you are!"

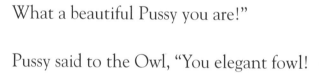

Pussy said to the Owl, "You elegant fowl!
How charmingly sweet you sing!
O let us be married! too long we have tarried:
But what shall we do for a ring?"
They sailed away for a year and a day,
To the land where the Bong-tree grows,
And there in a wood a Piggy-wig stood,
With a ring at the end of his nose,
　　His nose,
　　His nose,
With a ring at the end of his nose.

"Dear Pig, are you willing to sell for one shilling
Your ring?" Said the Piggy, "I will."
So they took it away, and were married next day
By the Turkey who lives on the hill.
They dined on mince, and slices of quince,
Which they ate with a runcible spoon;
And hand in hand, on the edge of the sand,
They danced by the light of the moon,
  The moon,
  The moon,
They danced by the light of the moon.

Edward Lear

Jabberwocky

'Twas brillig, and the slithy toves
Did gyre and gimble in the wabe:
All mimsy were the borogoves,
And the mome raths outgrabe.

"Beware the Jabberwock, my son!
The jaws that bite, the claws that catch!
Beware the Jubjub bird, and shun
The frumious Bandersnatch!"

He took his vorpal sword in hand:
Long time the manxome foe he sought –
So rested he by the Tumtum tree,
And stood awhile in thought.

And, as in uffish thought he stood,
The Jabberwock, with eyes of flame,
Came whiffling through the tulgey wood,
And burbled as it came!

One, two! One, two! And through and through
The vorpal blade went snicker-snack!
He left it dead, and with its head
He went galumphing back.

"And hast thou slain the Jabberwock?
Come to my arms, my beamish boy!
O frabjous day! Callooh! Callay!"
He chortled in his joy.

'Twas brillig, and the slithy toves
Did gyre and gimble in the wabe:
All mimsy were the borogoves,
And the mome raths outgrabe.

Lewis Carroll

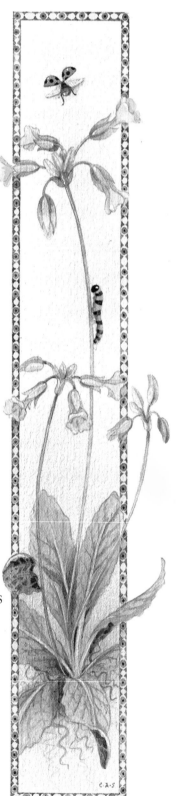

Hurt No Living Thing

Hurt no living thing;
Ladybird, nor butterfly,
Nor moth with dusty wing,
Nor cricket chirping cheerily,
Nor grasshopper so light of leap,
Nor dancing gnat, nor beetle fat,
Nor harmless worms that creep.

Christina Rossetti

Auguries of Innocence

To see a World in a Grain of Sand
And a Heaven in a Wild Flower,
Hold Infinity in the palm of your hand
And Eternity in an hour.

A Robin Red breast in a Cage
Puts all Heaven in a Rage.
A dove house fill'd with doves & Pigeons
Shudders Hell thro' all its regions.
A dog starv'd at his Master's Gate
Predicts the ruin of the State.
A Horse misus'd upon the Road
Calls to Heaven for Human blood.

Each outcry of the hunted Hare
A fiber from the Brain does tear.
A Skylark wounded in the wing,
A Cherubim does cease to sing.
The Game Cock clip'd & arm'd for fight
Does the Rising Sun affright.
Every Wolf's & Lion's howl
Raises from Hell a Human Soul.
The wild deer, wand'ring here & there,
Keeps the Human Soul from Care.
The Lamb misus'd breeds Public strife
And yet forgives the Butcher's Knife.
The Bat that flits at close of Eve
Has left the Brain that won't Believe.
The Owl that calls upon the Night
Speaks the Unbeliever's fright.
He who shall hurt the little Wren
Shall never be belov'd by Men.
He who the Ox to wrath has mov'd
Shall never be by Woman lov'd.
The wanton Boy that kills the Fly
Shall fell the Spider's enmity.
He who torments the Chafer's sprite
Weaves a Bower in endless Night.
The Catterpiller on the Leaf
Repeats to thee thy Mother's grief.
Kill not the Moth nor Butterfly,
For the Last Judgment draweth nigh.

William Blake

How Doth the Little Crocodile

How doth the little crocodile
Improve his shining tail;
And pour the waters of the Nile
On every golden scale!

How cheerfully he seems to grin,
How neatly spreads his claws,
And welcomes little fishes in,
With gently smiling jaws!

Lewis Carroll

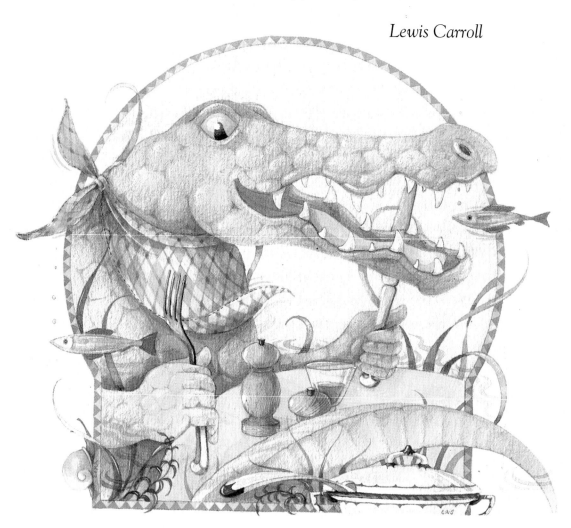

The Herring Loves the Merry Moonlight

The herring loves the merry moonlight,
The mackerel loves the wind,
But the oyster loves the dredging sang,
For they come of a gentle kind.

Sir Walter Scott

The Maldive Shark

About the Shark, phlegmatical one,
Pale sot of the Maldive sea,
The sleek little pilot-fish, azure and slim,
How alert in attendance be.
From his saw-pit of mouth, from his charnel of maw
They have nothing of harm to dread,
But liquidly glide on his ghastly flank
Or before his Gorgonian head;
Or luck in the port of serrated teeth
In white triple tiers of glittering gates,
And there find a haven when peril's abroad,
An asylum in jaws of the Fates!
They are friends; and friendly they guide him to prey,
Yet never partake of the treat –
Eyes and brains to the dotard lethargic and dull,
Pale ravener of horrible meat.

Herman Melville

My Cat Jeoffry

For I will consider my cat Jeoffry.
For he is the servant of the Living God,
    duly and daily serving him.
For at the first glance of the glory of God in
    the East he worships in his way.
For is this done by wreathing his body seven
    times round with elegant quickness.
For then he leaps up to catch the musk,
    which is the blessing of God upon his prayer.
For he rolls upon prank to work it in.
For having done duty and received blessing
    he begins to consider himself.
For this he performs in ten degrees.
For first he looks upon his fore-paws to see if
    they are clean.
For secondly he kicks up behind to clear away
    there.
For thirdly he works it upon stretch with the
    fore-paws extended.
For fourthly he sharpens his paws by wood.
For fifthly he washes himself.
For sixthly he rolls upon wash.
For seventhly he fleas himself, that he may not
    be interrupted upon the beat.
For eighthly he rubs himself against a post.
For ninthly he looks up for his instructions.
For tenthly he goes in quest of food.
For having considered God and himself he will
    consider his neighbor.

For if he meets another cat he will kiss her in
 kindness.
For when he takes his prey he plays with it to
 give it chance.
For one mouse in seven escapes by his
 dallying.
For when his day's work is done his business
 more properly begins.
For he keeps the Lord's watch in the night
 against the adversary.
For he counteracts the powers of darkness
 by his electrical skin & glaring eyes.
For he counteracts the Devil, who is death,
 by brisking about the life.
For in his morning orisons he loves the sun
 and the sun loves him.
For he is of the tribe of Tiger.
For the Cherub Cat is a term of the Angel Tiger.
For he has the subtlety and hissing of a serpent,
 which in goodness he suppresses.
For he will not do destruction, if he is well-fed,
 neither will he spit without provocation.
For he purrs in thankfulness, when God tells
 him he's a good Cat.
For he is an instrument for the children to learn
 benevolence upon.
For every house is incompleat without him &
 a blessing is lacking in the spirit.

Christopher Smart

The Owl

When cats run home and light is come,
And dew is cold upon the ground,
And the far-off stream is dumb,
And the whirring sail goes round,
And the whirring sail goes round;
Alone and warming his five wits,
The white owl in the belfry sits.

When merry milkmaids click the latch,
And rarely smells the new-mown hay,
And the cock hath sung beneath the thatch
Twice or thrice his roundelay,
Twice or thrice his roundelay;
Alone and warming his five wits,
The white owl in the belfry sits.

Alfred, Lord Tennyson

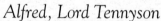

The Silver Swan

The silver swan, who living had no note,
When death approached, unlocked her silent throat,
Leaning her breast against the reedy shore,
Thus sung her first and last, and sung no more:
Farewell all joys! O death, come close mine eyes;
More geese than swans now live, more fools than wise.

Anonymous

The Eagle

He clasps the crag with crooked hands;
Close to the sun in lonely lands,
Ring'd with the azure world, he stands.

The wrinkled sea beneath him crawls;
He watches from his mountain walls,
And like a thunderbolt he falls.

Alfred, Lord Tennyson

The Tyger

Tyger! Tyger! burning bright
In the forests of the night,
What immortal hand or eye
Could frame thy fearful symmetry?

In what distant deeps or skies
Burnt the fire of thine eyes?
On what wings dare he aspire?
What the hand dare seize the fire?

And what shoulder, & what art,
Could twist the sinews of thy heart?
And when thy heart began to beat,
What dread hand? & what dread feet?

What the hammer? what the chain?
In what furnace was thy brain?
What the anvil? what dread grasp
Dare its deadly terrors clasp?

When the stars threw down their spears,
And water'd heaven with their tears,
Did he smile his work to see?
Did he who made the Lamb make thee?

Tyger! Tyger! burning bright
In the forests of the night,
What immortal hand or eye,
Could frame thy fearful symmetry?

William Blake

Weather and Seasons

Whether the Weather Be Fine

Whether the weather be fine
Or whether the weather be not,
Whether the weather be cold
Or whether the weather be hot,
We'll weather the weather
Whatever the weather,
Whether we like it or not.

Anonymous

It's Raining, It's Pouring

It's raining, it's pouring,
The old man is snoring;
He went to bed and bumped his head
And couldn't get up in the morning!

Anonymous

The Rainbow

Boats sail on the rivers,
And ships sail on the seas;
But clouds that sail across the sky
Are prettier far than these.

There are bridges on the rivers,
As pretty as you please;
But the bow that bridges heaven,
And overtops the trees,
And builds a road from earth to sky,
Is prettier far than these.

Christina Rossetti

The Wind

Who has seen the wind?
Neither I nor you;
But when the leaves hang trembling
The wind is passing through.

Who has seen the wind?
Neither you nor I;
But when the trees bow down their heads
The wind is passing by.

Christina Rossetti

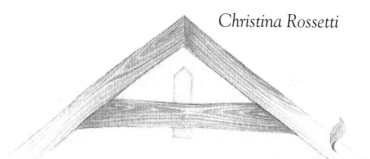

The North Wind Doth Blow

The north wind doth blow,
And we shall have snow,
And what will poor robin do then,
Poor thing?

He'll sit in a barn,
And keep himself warm,
And hide his head under his wing,
Poor thing.

Anonymous

Windy Nights

Whenever the moon and stars are set,
 Whenever the wind is high,
All night long in the dark and wet,
 A man goes riding by.
Late in the night when the fires are out,
Why does he gallop and gallop about?

Whenever the trees are crying aloud,
 And ships are tossed at sea,
By, on the highway, low and loud,
 By at the gallop goes he.
By at the gallop he goes, and then
By he comes back at the gallop again.

Robert Louis Stevenson

The Human Seasons

Four seasons fill the measure of the year;
There are four seasons in the mind of man:
He has his lusty Spring, when fancy clear
Takes in all beauty with an easy span:

He has his Summer, when luxuriously
Spring's honey'd cud of youthful thought he loves
To ruminate, and by such dreaming nigh
His nearest unto heaven: quiet coves

His soul has in its Autumn, when his wings
He furleth close; contented so to look
On mists in idleness – to let fair things
Pass by unheeded as a threshold brook:

He has his Winter too of pale misfeature,
Or else he would forgo his mortal nature.

John Keats

Winter

When icicles hang by the wall,
And Dick the shepherd blows his nail,
And Tom bears logs into the hall,
And milk comes frozen home in pail;
When blood is nipped, and ways be foul,
Then nightly sings the staring owl.
Tu-whit, tu-who! a merry note,
While greasy Joan doth keel the pot.

When all aloud the wind doth blow,
And coughing drowns the parson's saw,
And birds sit brooding in the snow,
And Marian's nose looks red and raw,
When roasted crabs hiss in the bowl,
Then nightly sings the staring owl,
Tu-whit, tu-who! a merry note,
While greasy Joan doth keel the pot.

William Shakespeare

Spring

Sound the Flute!
Now it's mute.
Birds delight
Day and Night;
Nightingale
In the dale,
Lark in Sky,
Merrily,
Merrily, Merrily, to welcome in the Year.

Little Boy,
Full of joy;
Little Girl,
Sweet and small;
Cock does crow,
So do you;
Merry voice,
Infant noise,
Merrily, Merrily, to welcome in the Year.

Little Lamb,
Here I am;
Come and lick
My white neck;
Let me pull
Your soft Wool;
Let me kiss
Your soft face:
Merrily, Merrily, we welcome in the Year.

William Blake

From *Rain in Summer*

How beautiful is the rain!
After the dust and heat,
In the broad and fiery street,
In the narrow lane,
How beautiful is the rain!

How it clatters along the roofs,
Like the tramp of hoofs!
How it gushes and struggles out
From the throat of the overflowing spout!

Across the window-pane
It pours and pours;
And swift and wide,
With a muddy tide,
Like a river down the gutter roars
The rain, the welcome rain!

Henry Wadsworth Longfellow

Fall, Leaves, Fall

Fall, leaves, fall: die, flowers, away;
Lengthen night and shorten day,
Every leaf speaks bliss to me
Fluttering from the autumn tree.
I shall smile when wreaths of snow
Blossom where the rose should grow;
I shall sing when night's decay
Ushers in a drearier day.

Emily Brontë

The Year's at the Spring

The year's at the spring
And day's at the morn;
Morning's at seven;
The hill-side's dew-pearled;
The lark's on the wing;
The snail's on the thorn:
God's in his heaven –
All's right with the world!

Robert Browning

BRIGHT
and
BEAUTIFUL

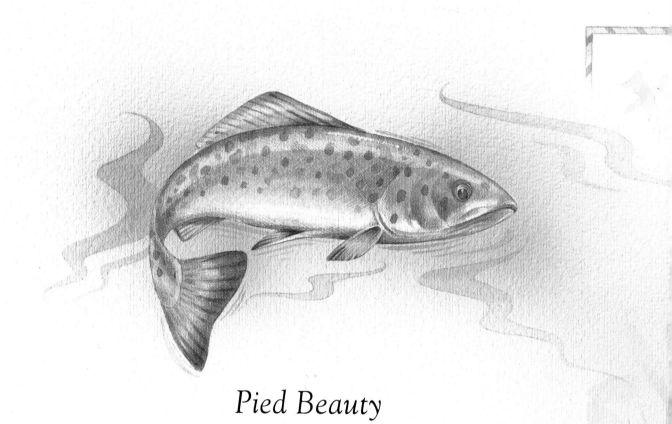

Pied Beauty

Glory be to God for dappled things –
For skies of couple-color as a brinded cow;
For rose-moles all in stipple upon trout that swim;
Fresh-firecoal chestnut-falls; finches' wings;
Landscape plotted and pieced – fold, fallow, and plough;
And all trades, their gear and tackle and trim.

All things counter, original, spare, strange;
Whatever is fickle, freckled (who knows how?)
With swift, slow; sweet, sour; adazzle, dim;
He fathers-forth whose beauty is past change:
                                        Praise him

Gerard Manley Hopkins

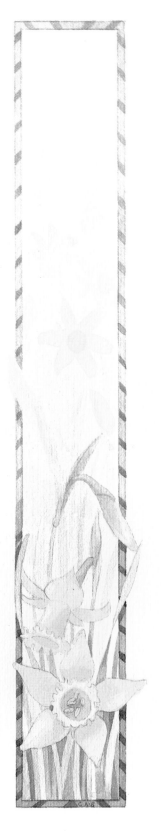

Daffodils

I wandered lonely as a cloud
    That floats on high o'er vales and hills,
When all at once I saw a crowd,
    A host, of golden daffodils;
Beside the lake, beneath the trees,
Fluttering and dancing in the breeze.

Continuous as the stars that shine
    And twinkle on the Milky Way,
They stretched in never-ending line
    Along the margin of a bay:
Ten thousand saw I at a glance,
Tossing their heads in sprightly dance.

The waves beside them danced, but they
    Out-did the sparkling waves in glee:
A poet could not but be gay,
    In such a jocund company:
I gazed – and gazed – but little thought
What wealth the show to me had brought:

For oft, when on my couch I lie
    In vacant or in pensive mood,
They flash upon that inward eye
    Which is the bliss of solitude;
And then my heart with pleasure fills,
And dances with the daffodils.

William Wordsworth

My Shadow

I have a little shadow that goes in and out with me,
And what can be the use of him is more than I can see.
He is very, very like me from the heels up to the head;
And I see him jump before me, when I jump into my bed.

The funniest thing about him is the way he likes to grow –
Not at all like proper children, which is always very slow;
For he sometimes shoots up taller like an india-rubber ball,
And he sometimes gets so little that there's none of him at all.

He hasn't got a notion of how children ought to play,
And can only make a fool of me in every sort of way.
He stays so close behind me he's a coward you can see;
I'd think shame to stick to nursie as that shadow sticks to me!

One morning, very early, before the sun was up,
I rose and found the shining dew on every buttercup;
But my lazy little shadow, like an arrant sleepy-head,
Had stayed at home behind me and was fast asleep in bed.

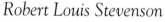

Robert Louis Stevenson

The Ecchoing Green

The sun does arise;
And make happy the skies.
The merry bells ring
To welcome the Spring;
The skylark and thrush,
The birds of the bush,
Sing louder around
To the bells' chearful sound,
While our sports shall be seen
On the Ecchoing Green.

Old John, with white hair,
Does laugh away care,
Sitting under the oak,
Among the old folk.
They laugh at our play,
And soon they all say:
"Such, such were the joys
When we all, girls & boys,
In our youth time were seen
On the Ecchoing Green."

Till the little ones, weary,
No more can be merry;
The sun does descend,
And our sports have an end.
Round the laps of their mothers
Many sisters and brothers,
Like birds in their nest,
Are ready for rest,
And sport no more seen
On the darkening Green.

William Blake

She Walks in Beauty

She walks in beauty, like the night
    Of cloudless climes and starry skies;
And all that's best of dark and bright
    Meet in her aspect and her eyes:
Thus mellowed to that tender light
    Which heaven to gaudy day denies.

One shade the more, one ray the less,
    Had half impaired the nameless grace
Which waves in every raven tress,
    Or softly lightens o'er her face;
Where thoughts serenely sweet express
    How pure, how dear their dwelling-place.

And on that cheek, and o'er that brow,
    So soft, so calm, yet eloquent,
The smiles that win, the tints that glow,
    But tell of days in goodness spent,
A mind at peace with all below,
    A heart whose love is innocent.

George Gordon, Lord Byron

Shall I Compare Thee to a Summer's Day?

Shall I compare thee to a summer's day?
　　Thou art more lovely and more temperate:
Rough winds do shake the darling buds of May,
　　And summer's lease hath all too short a date:
Sometime too hot the eye of heaven shines,
　　And often is his gold complexion dimmed;
And every fair from fair sometime declines,
　　By chance, or nature's changing course untrimmed;
But thy eternal summer shall not fade,
　　Nor lose possession of that fair thou owest,
Nor shall Death brag thou wanderest in his shade,
　　When in eternal lines to time thou growest;
So long as men can breathe, or eyes can see,
So long lives this, and this gives life to thee.

William Shakespeare

45

Blow, Bugle, Blow

The splendor falls on castle walls
    And snowy summits old in story:
The long light shakes across the lakes,
    And the wild cataract leaps in glory.
Blow, bugle, blow, set the wild echoes flying,
Blow, bugle; answer, echoes, dying, dying, dying.

O hark, O hear! how thin and clear,
    And thinner, clearer, farther going!
O sweet and far from cliff and scar
    The horns of Elfland faintly blowing!
Blow, let us hear the purple glens replying:
Blow, bugle; answer, echoes, dying, dying, dying.

O love, they die in yon rich sky,
    They faint on hill or field or river:
Our echoes roll from soul to soul,
    And grow for ever and for ever.
Blow, bugle, blow, set the wild echoes flying,
And answer, echoes, answer, dying, dying, dying.

Alfred, Lord Tennyson

DREAMS
and
WONDERS

Kubla Khan

In Xanadu did Kubla Khan
 A stately pleasure-dome decree:
Where Alph, the sacred river, ran
Through caverns measureless to man
 Down to a sunless sea.
So twice five miles of fertile ground
 With walls and towers were girdled round:
And there were gardens bright with sinuous rills
Where blossomed many an incense-bearing tree;
And here were forests ancient as the hills,
Enfolding sunny spots of greenery.

But O, that deep romantic chasm which slanted
Down the green hill athwart a cedarn cover!
A savage place! as holy and enchanted
As e'er beneath a waning moon was haunted
By woman wailing for her demon-lover!
And from this chasm, with ceaseless turmoil seething,
As if this earth in fast thick pants were breathing,
A mighty fountain momently was forced;
Amid whose swift half-intermitted burst
Huge fragments vaulted like rebounding hail,
Or chaffy grain beneath the thresher's flail:
And 'mid these dancing rocks at once and ever
It flung up momently the sacred river.
Five miles meandering with a mazy motion
Through wood and dale the sacred river ran,
Then reached the caverns measureless to man,
And sank in tumult to a lifeless ocean:
And 'mid this tumult Kubla heard from far
Ancestral voices prophesying war!

The shadow of the dome of pleasure
    Floated midway on the waves;
Where was heard the mingled measure
    From the fountain and the caves.
It was a miracle of rare device,
A sunny pleasure-dome with caves of ice!

A damsel with a dulcimer
    In a vision once I saw:
It was an Abyssinian maid,
    And on her dulcimer she played,
Singing of Mount Abora.
Could I revive within me,
    Her symphony and song,
To such a deep delight 'twould win me,
That with music loud and long,
I would build that dome in air,
That sunny dome! those caves of ice!
And all who heard should see them there,
And all should cry, Beware! Beware!
His flashing eyes, his floating hair!
    Weave a circle round him thrice,
        And close your eyes with holy dread,
    For he on honey-dew hath fed,
        And drunk the milk of Paradise.

Samuel Taylor Coleridge

The Fairies

Up the airy mountain,
Down the rushy glen,
We daren't go a-hunting
For fear of little men;
Wee folk, good folk,
Trooping all together;
Green jacket, red cap,
And white owl's feather!

Down along the rocky shore
Some make their home,
They live on crispy pancakes
Of yellow tide-foam;
Some in the reeds
Of the black mountain lake,
With frogs for their watch-dogs,
All night awake.

High on the hill-top
The old King sits;
He is now so old and gray
He's right lost his wits.
With a bridge of white mist
Columbkill he crosses,
On his stately journeys
From Slieveleague to Rosses;
Or going up with music
On cold starry nights
To sup with the Queen
Of the gay Northern Lights.

50

They stole little Bridget
For seven years long;
When she came down again
Her friends were all gone.
They took her lightly back,
Between the night and morrow,
They thought that she was fast asleep,
But she was dead with sorrow.
They have kept her ever since
Deep within the lake,
On a bed of flag-leaves,
Watching till she wake.

By the craggy hill-side,
Through the mosses bare,
They have planted thorn-trees
For pleasure here and there.
Is any man so daring
As dig them up in spite,
He shall find their sharpest thorns
In his bed at night.

Up the airy mountain,
Down the rushy glen,
We daren't go a-hunting
For fear of little men;
Wee folk, good folk,
Trooping all together;
Green jacket, red cap,
And white owl's feather!

William Allingham

La Belle Dame Sans Merci

O what can ail thee, knight-at-arms,
Alone and palely loitering?
The sedge has wither'd from the lake,
And no birds sing.

O what can ail thee, knight-at-arms,
So haggard and so woe-begone?
The squirrel's granary is full,
And the harvest's done.

I see a lily on thy brow,
With anguish moist and fever dew;
And on thy cheeks a fading rose
Fast withereth too.

I met a lady in the meads,
Full beautiful – a faery's child,
Her hair was long, her foot was light,
And her eyes were wild.

I made a garland for her head,
And bracelets too, and fragrant zone;
She look'd at me as she did love,
And made sweet moan.

I set her on my pacing steed,
And nothing else saw all day long;
For sidelong would she bend, and sing
A faery's song.

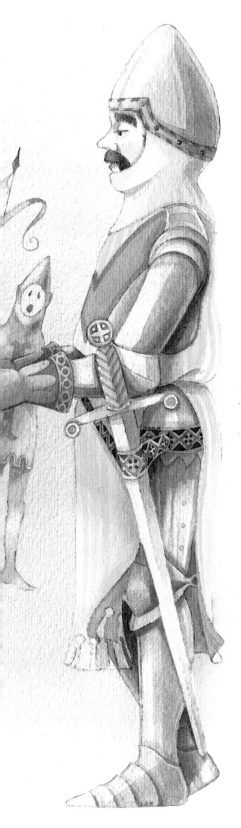

She found me roots of relish sweet,
And honey wild, and manna dew,
And sure in language strange she said –
"I love thee true".

She took me to her elfin grot,
And there she wept and sigh'd full sore,
And there I shut her wild wild eyes
With kisses four.

And there she lulled me asleep
And there I dream'd – Ah! woe betide!
The latest dream I ever dream'd
On the cold hill side.

I saw pale kings and princes too,
Pale warriors, death-pale were they all;
They cried – "La Belle Dame sans Merci
Hath thee in thrall!"

I saw their starved lips in the gloam,
With horrid warning gaped wide,
And I awoke and found me here,
On the cold hill's side.

And this is why I sojourn here
Alone and palely loitering,
Though the sedge has wither'd from the lake,
And no birds sing.

John Keats

I Saw a Peacock

I saw a peacock with a fiery tail
I saw a blazing comet drop down hail
I saw a cloud wrapped with ivy round
I saw an oak creep upon the ground
I saw a pismire swallow up a whale
I saw the sea brimful of ale
I saw a Venice glass full fifteen feet deep
I saw a well full of men's tears that weep
I saw red eyes all of a flaming fire
I saw a house bigger than the moon and higher
I saw the sun at twelve o'clock at night
I saw the man that saw this wondrous sight.

Anonymous

A Child's Thought

At seven, when I go to bed,
I find such pictures in my head:
Castles with dragons prowling round,
Gardens where magic fruits are found;
Fair ladies prisoned in a tower,
Or lost in an enchanted bower;
While gallant horsemen ride by streams
That border all this land of dreams
I find, so clearly in my head
At seven, when I go to bed.

Robert Louis Stevenson

Songs
of
The Sea

Full Fathom Five

Full fathom five they father lies;
    Of his bones are coral made;
Those are pearls that were his eyes:
    Nothing of him that doth fade,
But doth suffer a sea-change
Into something rich and strange:
Sea nymphs hourly ring his knell.
                 Ding-dong!
Hark! now I hear them,
            Ding-dong, bell!

William Shakespeare

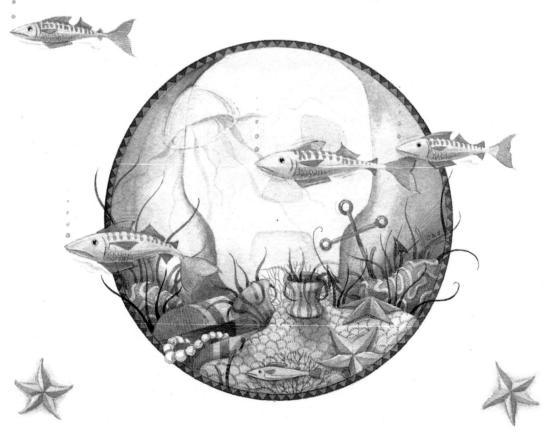

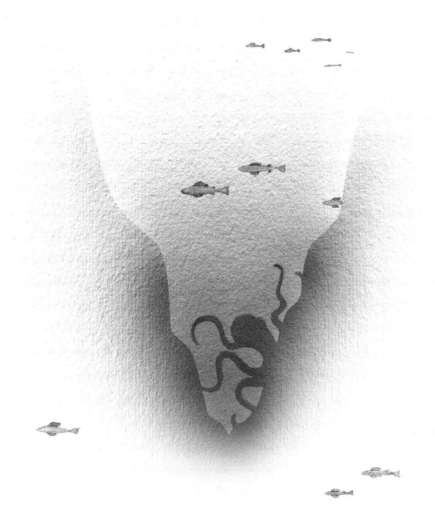

What Are Heavy?

What are heavy? sea-sand and sorrow:
What are brief? today and tomorrow:
What are frail? Spring blossoms and youth:
What are deep? the ocean and truth.

Christina Rossetti

I Started Early

I started Early – Took my Dog –
And visited the Sea –
The Mermaids in the Basement
Came out to look at me –

And Frigates – in the Upper Floor
Extended Hempen Hands –
Presuming Me to be a Mouse –
Aground – upon the Sands –

But no Man moved Me – till the Tide
Went past my simple Shoe –
And past my Apron – and my Belt
And past my Bodice – too –

And made as He would eat me up –
As wholly as a Dew
Upon a Dandelion's Sleeve –
And then – I started – too –

And He – He followed – close behind –
I felt His Silver Heel
Upon my Ankle – Then my Shoes
Would overflow with Pearl –

Until We met the Solid Town –
No One He seemed to know –
And bowing – with a Mighty look –
At me – The Sea withdrew –

Emily Dickinson

58

O Captain! My Captain!

O Captain! my Captain! our fearful trip is done,
The ship has weather'd every rack, the prize we sought is won,
The port is near, the bells I hear, the people all exulting,
While follow eyes the steady keel, the vessel grim and daring;
 But O heart! heart! heart!
 O the bleeding drops of red,
  Where on the deck my Captain lies,
   Fallen cold and dead.

O Captain! my Captain! rise up and hear the bells;
Rise up – for you the flag is flung – for you the bugle trills,
For you bouquets and ribbon'd wreaths – for you the shores a-crowding,
For you they call, the swaying mass, their eager faces turning;
 Here Captain! dear father!
 This arm beneath your head!
  It is some dream that on the deck,
   You've fallen cold and dead.

My Captain does not answer, his lips are pale and still,
My father does not feel my arm, he has no pulse nor will,
The ship is anchor'd safe and sound, its voyage closed and done,
From fearful trip the victor ship comes in with object won;
 Exult O shores, and ring O bells!
 But I with mournful tread,
  Walk the deck my Captain lies,
   Fallen cold and dead.

Walt Whitman

Break, Break, Break

Break, break, break,
    On thy cold gray stones, O Sea!
And I would that my tongue could utter
    The thoughts that arise in me.

O well for the fisherman's boy,
    That he shouts with his sister at play!
O well for the sailor lad,
    That he sings in his boat on the bay!

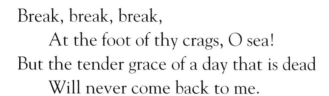

And the stately ships go on
     To their haven under the hill;
But O for the touch of a vanish'd hand,
     And the sound of a voice that is still!

Break, break, break,
     At the foot of thy crags, O sea!
But the tender grace of a day that is dead
     Will never come back to me.

Alfred, Lord Tennyson

Meeting at Night

The gray sea and the long black land;
And the yellow half-moon large and low;
And the startled little waves that leap
In fiery ringlets from their sleep,
As I gain the cove with pushing prow,
And quench its speed i' the slushy sand.

Then a mile of warm sea-scented beach;
Three fields to cross till a farm appears;
A tap at the pane, the quick sharp scratch
And blue spurt of a lighted match,
And a voice less loud, thro' its joys and fears,
Than the two hearts beating each to each!

Robert Browning

64

TALES
of
TRAVEL

Ozymandias

I met a traveler from an antique land
Who said: Two vast and trunkless legs of stone
Stand in the desert ... Near them, on the sand,
Half sunk, a shattered visage lies, whose frown,
And wrinkled lip, and sneer of cold command,
Tell that its sculptor well those passions read
Which yet survive, stamped on these lifeless things,
The hand that mocked them, and the heart that fed:
And on the pedestal these words appear:
"My name is Ozymandias, king of kings:
Look on my works, ye Mighty, and despair!"
Nothing beside remains. Round the decay
Of that colossal wreck, boundless and bare
The lone and level sands stretch far away.

Percy Bysshe Shelley

Where Lies the Land?

Where lies the land to which the ship would go?
Far, far ahead, is all her seamen know.
And where the land she travels from? Away,
Far, far behind, is all that they can say.

On sunny noons upon the deck's smooth face,
Linked arm in arm, how pleasant here to pace;
Or, o'er the stern reclining, watch below
The foaming wake far widening as we go.

On stormy nights when wild north-westers rave,
How proud a thing to fight with wind and wave!
The dripping sailor on the reeling mast
Exults to bear, and scorns to wish it past.

Where lies the land to which the ship would go?
Far, far ahead, is all her seamen know.
And where the land she travels from? Away,
Far, far behind, is all that they can say.

Arthur Hugh Clough

Eldorado

Gaily bedight,
A gallant knight,
In sunshine and in shadow,
Had journeyed long,
Singing a song,
In search of Eldorado.

But he grew old –
This knight so bold –
And o'er his heart a shadow
Fell, as he found
No spot of ground
That looked like Eldorado.

68

And, as his strength
Failed him at length,
He met a pilgrim shadow –
"Shadow," said he,
"Where can it be –
This land of Eldorado?"

"Over the Mountains
Of the Moon,
Down the Valley of the Shadow,
Ride, boldly ride,"
The shade replied,
"If you seek for Eldorado!"

Edgar Allan Poe

69

Foreign Lands

Up into the cherry-tree
Who should climb but little me?
I held the trunk with both my hands
And looked abroad on foreign lands.

I saw the next-door garden lie,
Adorned with flowers before my eye,
And many pleasant places more
That I had never seen before.

I saw the dimpling river pass
And be the sky's blue looking-glass;
The dusty roads go up and down
With people tramping in to town.

If I could find a higher tree
Farther and farther I should see,
To where the grown-up river slips
Into the sea among the ships,

To where the roads on either hand
Lead onward into fairy land,
Where all the children dine at five,
And all the playthings come alive.

Robert Louis Stevenson

Uphill

Does the road wind uphill all the way?
Yes, to the very end.
Will the day's journey take the whole long day?
From morn to night, my friend.

But is there for the night a resting-place?
A roof for when the slow, dark hours begin.
May not the darkness hide it from my face?
You cannot miss that inn.

Shall I meet other wayfarers at night?
Those who have gone before.
Then must I knock, or call when just in sight?
They will not keep you waiting at that door.

Shall I find comfort, travel-sore and weak?
Of labor you shall find the sum.
Will there be beds for me and all who seek?
Yea, beds for all who come.

Christina Rossetti

Travel

I should like to rise and go
Where the golden apples grow;
Where below another sky
Parrot islands anchored lie,
And, watched by cockatoos and goats,
Lonely Crusoes building boats;
Where in sunshine reaching out
Eastern cities, miles about,
Are with mosque and minaret
Among sandy gardens set,
And the rich goods from near and far
Hang for sale in the bazaar;
Where the Great Wall round China goes,
And on one side the desert blows,
And with bell and voice and drum,
Cities on the other hum;

Where are forests, hot as fire,
Wide as England, tall as a spire,
Full of apes and coco-nuts
And the negro hunters' huts;
Where the knotty crocodile
Lies and blinks in the Nile,
And the red flamingo flies
Hunting fish before his eyes;

Where in jungles, near and far,
Man-devouring tigers are,
Lying close and giving ear
Lest the hunt be drawing near,
Or a comer-by be seen
Swinging in a palanquin;
Where among the desert sands
Some deserted city stands,

All its children, sweep and prince,
Grown to manhood ages since,
Not a foot in street or house,
Not a stir of child or mouse,
And when kindly falls the night,
In all the town no spark of light.
There I'll come when I'm a man
With a camel caravan;
Light a fire in the gloom
Of some dusty dining-room;
See the pictures on the walls,
Heroes, fights and festivals;
And in a corner find the toys
Of the old Egyptian boys.

Robert Louis Stevenson

From a Railway Carriage

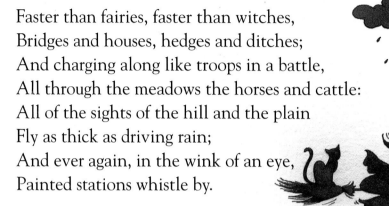

Faster than fairies, faster than witches,
Bridges and houses, hedges and ditches;
And charging along like troops in a battle,
All through the meadows the horses and cattle:
All of the sights of the hill and the plain
Fly as thick as driving rain;
And ever again, in the wink of an eye,
Painted stations whistle by.

Here is a child who clambers and scrambles,
All by himself and gathering brambles;
Here is a tramp who stands and gazes;
And there is the green for stringing the daisies!
Here is a cart run away in the road
Lumping along with man and load;
And here is a mill, and there is a river:
Each a glimpse and gone for ever!

Robert Louis Stevenson

CHILDHOOD

Little Orphant Annie

Little Orphant Annie's come to our house to stay,
An' wash the cups and saucers up, an' brush the crumbs away,
An' shoo the chickens off the porch, an' dust the hearth, an' sweep,
An' make the fire, an' bake the bread, an' earn her board-an'-keep;
An' all us other children, when the supper things is done,
We set around the kitchen fire an' has the mostest fun
A-list'nin' to the witch-tales 'at Annie tells about,
An' the Gobble-uns 'at gits you
    Ef you
        Don't
            Watch
              Out!

Wunst they was a little boy wouldn't say his prayers,–
An' when he went to bed at night, away up-stairs,
His Mammy heerd him holler, an' his Daddy heerd him bawl,
An' when they turn't the kivvers down, he wazn't there at all!
An' they seeked him in the rafter-room, an' cubby-hole, an' press,
An' seeked him up the chimbly-flue, an' ever'wheres, I guess;
But all they ever found wuz thist his pants an' round-about: –
An' the Gobble-uns 'll git you
    Ef you
        Don't
            Watch
              Out!

An' one time a little girl 'ud allus laugh and grin,
An' make fun of ever'one, an' all her blood-an'-kin;
An' wunst, when they wuz "company," an' ole folks wuz there,
She mocked 'em an' shocked 'em, an' said she didn't care!
An' thist as she kicked her heels, an' turn't to run an' hide,
They wuz two great big Black Things a-standin' by her side,
An' they snatched her through the ceilin' 'fore she knowed what she's
    about!
An' the Gobble-uns 'll git you
    Ef you
        Don't
            Watch
                Out!

An' little Orphant Annie says, when the blaze is blue,
An' the lamp wick sputters, an' the wind goes *woo-oo!*
An' you hear the crickets quit, an' the moon is gray,
An' the lightnin'-bugs in dew is all squenched away, –
You better mind yer parunts, an' yer teachers fond an' dear,
An' churish them 'at loves you, an' dry the orphant's tear,
An' he'p the pore an' needy ones 'at clusters all about,
Er the Gobble-uns 'll git you
    Ef you
        Don't
            Watch
                Out!

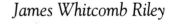

James Whitcomb Riley

Monday's Child

Monday's child is fair of face,
Tuesday's child is full of grace,
Wednesday's child is full of woe,
Thursday's child has far to go,
Friday's child is loving and giving,
Saturday's child works hard for his living,
And the child that is born on the Sabbath day
Is bonny and blithe, and good and gay.

Anonymous

A Child's Grace

Here a little child I stand
Heaving up my either hand;
Cold as paddocks though they be,
Here I lift them up to Thee,
For a benison to fall
On our meat and on us all.
                    Amen.

Robert Herrick

I Remember, I Remember

I remember, I remember,
The house where I was born,
The little window where the sun
Came peeping in at morn;
He never came a wink too soon,
Nor brought too long a day,
But now, I often wish the night
Had borne my breath away!

I remember, I remember,
The roses, red and white,
The violets, and the lily-cups,
Those flowers made of light!
The lilacs where the robin built,
And where my brother set
The laburnum on his birthday, –
The tree is living yet!

I remember, I remember,
Where I was used to swing,
And thought the air must rush as fresh
To swallows on the wing;
My spirit flew in feathers then,
That is so heavy now,
And summer pools could hardly cool
The fever on my brow!

I remember, I remember,
The fir trees dark and high;
I used to think their slender tops
Were close against the sky:
It was a childish ignorance,
But now 'tis little joy
To know I'm farther off from Heav'n
Than when I was a boy.

Thomas Hood

Swing, Swing

Swing, swing,
Sing, sing,
Here! my throne and I am a king!
Swing, swing,
Sing, sing,
Farewell, earth, for I'm on the wing!

Low, high,
Here I fly,
Like a bird through sunny sky;
Free, free,
Over the lea,
Over the mountain, over the sea!

Soon, soon,
Afternoon,
Over the sunset, over the moon;
Far, far,
Over all bar,
Sweeping on from star to star!

No, no,
Low, low,
Sweeping daisies with my toe.
Slow, slow,
To and fro,
Slow – slow – slow – slow.

William Allingham

Good and Bad Children

Children, you are very little,
And your bones are very brittle;
If you would grow great and stately,
You must try to walk sedately.

You must still be bright and quiet,
And content with simple diet;
And remain, through all bewild'ring.
Innocent and honest children.

Happy hearts and happy faces,
Happy play in grassy places –
That was how, in ancient ages,
Children grew to kings and sages.

But the unkind and the unruly,
And the sort to eat unduly,
They must never hope for glory –
Theirs is quite a different story!

Cruel children, crying babies,
All grow up as geese and gabies,
Hated, as their age increases,
By their nephews and their nieces.

Robert Louis Stevenson

At the End
of
The Day

Escape at Bedtime

The lights from the parlor and kitchen shone out
    Through the blinds and the windows and bars;
And high overhead and all moving about,
    There were thousands of millions of stars.
There ne'er were such thousands of leaves on a tree,
    Nor of people in church or the Park,
As the crowds of the stars looked down upon me,
    And that glittered and winked in the dark.

The Dog, and the Plough, and the Hunter, and all,
    And the star of the sailor, and Mars,
These shone in the sky, and the pail by the wall
    Would be half full of water and stars.
They saw me at last, and they chased me with cries,
    And they soon had me packed into bed;
But the glory kept shining and bright in my eyes,
    And the stars going round in my head.

Robert Louis Stevenson

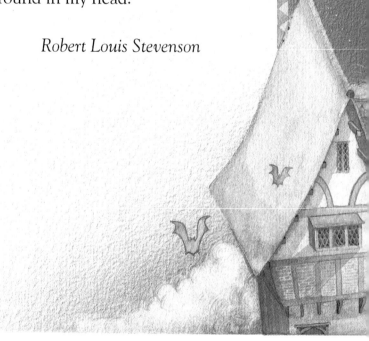

Bed in Summer

In winter I get up at night
And dress by yellow candle-light.
In summer, quite the other way,
I have to go to bed by day.

I have to go to bed and see
The birds still hopping on the tree,
Or hear the grown-up people's feet
Still going past me in the street.

And does it not seem hard to you,
When all the sky is clear and blue,
And I should like so much to play,
To have to go to bed by day?

Robert Louis Stevenson

Is the Moon Tired?

Is the moon tired? She looks so pale
    Within her misty veil;
She scales the sky from east to west,
    And takes no rest.

Before the coming of the night
    The moon shows papery white;
Before the dawning of the day
    She fades away.

Christina Rossetti

Wynken, Blynken, and Nod

Wynken, Blynken, and Nod one night
Sailed off in a wooden shoe –
Sailed on a river of crystal light,
Into a sea of dew.
"Where are you going, and what do you wish?"
The old moon asked the three.
"We have come to fish for the herring fish
That live in this beautiful sea;
Nets of silver and gold have we!"
    Said Wynken,
    Blynken,
    And Nod.

The old moon laughed and sang a song
As they rocked in the wooden shoe,
And the wind that sped them all night long
Ruffled the waves of dew.
The little stars were the herring fish
That lived in that beautiful sea –
"Now cast your nets wherever you wish –
Never afeard are we";
So cried the stars to the fishermen three:
    Wynken,
    Blynken,
    And Nod.

All night long their nets they threw
To the stars in the twinkling foam –
Then down from the skies came the wooden shoe,
Bringing the fishermen home;
'Twas all so pretty a sail it seemed
As if it could not be,
And some folks thought 'twas a dream they'd dreamed
Of sailing that beautiful sea –
But I shall name you the fishermen three:
    Wynken,
    Blynken,
    And Nod.

Wynken and Blynken are two little eyes,
And Nod is a little head,
And the wooden shoe that sailed the skies
Is a wee one's trundle-bed.
So shut your eyes while mother sings
Of wonderful sights that be,
And you shall see the beautiful things
As you rock in the misty sea,
Where the old shoe rocked the fishermen three:
    Wynken,
    Blynken,
    And Nod.

Eugene Field

Star Light, Star Bright

Star light, star bright,
First star I see tonight,
I wish I may, I wish I might,
Have the wish I wish tonight.

Anonymous

How Many Miles to Babylon?

How many miles to Babylon?
Three score miles and ten.
Can I get there by candlelight?
Yes, and back again.
If your heels are nimble and light,
You may get there by candlelight.

Anonymous

Hush Little Baby

Hush little baby, don't say a word,
Papa's going to buy you a mockingbird.

If that mockingbird won't sing,
Papa's going to buy you a diamond ring.

If that diamond ring turns brass,
Papa's going to buy you a looking glass.

If that looking glass gets broke,
Papa's going to buy you a billy goat.

If that billy goat won't pull,
Papa's going to buy you a cart and bull.

If that cart and bull fall down,
You'll still be the sweetest little baby in town.

Anonymous

Sleep, Baby, Sleep!

Sleep, baby, sleep!
Your father herds his sheep:
Your mother shakes the little tree
From which fall pretty dreams on thee;
Sleep, baby, sleep!

Sleep, baby, sleep!
The heavens are white with sheep:
For they are lambs – those stars so bright:
And the moon's shepherd of the night;
Sleep, baby, sleep!

Sleep, baby, sleep!
And I'll give thee a sheep,
Which, with its golden bell, shall be
A little play-fellow for thee;
Sleep, baby, sleep!

Sleep, baby, sleep!
And bleat not like a sheep,
Or else the shepherd's angry dog
Will come and bite my naughty rogue;
Sleep, baby, sleep!

Sleep, baby, sleep!
Go out and herd the sheep,
Go out, you barking black dog, go,
And waken not my baby so;
Sleep, baby, sleep!

Anonymous

LOVE and ADVENTURE

Robin Hood

In Sherwood lived stout Robin Hood,
    An Archer great none greater.
His bow and shafts were sure and good,
    Yet Cupid's were much better.
Robin could shoot at many a Hart and miss,
    Cupid at first could hit a heart of his.
        Hey jolly Robin,
        Hoe jolly Robin,
        Hey jolly Robin Hood,
        Love finds out me
        As well as thee
        To follow me to the green wood.

A noble thief was Robin Hood,
    Wise was he could deceive him,
Yet Marian in his bravest mood
    Could of his heart bereave him,
No greater thief lies hidden under skies
    Than beauty closely lodged in women's eyes.
      Hey jolly Robin,
      Hoe jolly Robin,
      Hey jolly Robin Hood,
      Love finds out me
      As well as thee
      To follow me to the green wood.

Robert Jones

A Red, Red Rose

My love is like a red, red rose
    That's newly sprung in June:
My love is like the melody
    That's sweetly played in tune.

As fair art thou, my bonnie lass,
    So deep in love am I:
And I will love thee still, my dear,
    Till a' the seas gang dry.

Till a' the seas gang dry, my dear,
    And the rocks melt wi' the sun:
And I will love thee still, my dear,
    While the sands o' life shall run.

And fare thee weel, my only love,
    And fare thee weel a while!
And I will come again, my love,
    Thou' it were ten thousand mile.

Robert Burns

A Birthday

My heart is like a singing bird
    Whose nest is in a watered shoot;
My heart is like an apple-tree
    Whose boughs are bent with thickset fruit;
My heart is like a rainbow shell
    That paddles in a halcyon sea;
My heart is gladder than all these
    Because my love is come to me.

Raise me a dais of silk and down;
    Hang it with vair and purple dyes;
Carve it in doves and pomegranates,
    And peacocks with a hundred eyes;
Work it in gold and silver grapes,
    In leaves and silver fleurs-de-lys;
Because the birthday of my life
    Is come, my love is come to me.

Christina Rossetti

Lochinvar

O, young Lochinvar is come out of the west,
Through all the wide Border his steed was the best;
And save his good broadsword he weapons had none,
He rode all unarmed, and he rode all alone.
So faithful in love, and so dauntless in war,
There never was knight like the young Lochinvar.

He stayed not for brake, and he stopped not for stone,
He swam the Eske river where ford there was none;
But ere he alighted at Netherby gate,
The bride had consented, the gallant came late:
For a laggard in love, and a dastard in war,
Was to wed the fair Ellen of brave Lochinvar.

So boldly he entered the Netherby Hall,
Among bride's-men, and kinsmen, and brothers, and all:
Then spoke the bride's father, his hand on his sword,
(For the poor craven bridegroom said never a word)
"O come ye in peace here, or come ye in war,
Or to dance at our bridal, young Lord Lochinvar?"

"I long wooed your daughter, my suit you denied;—
Love swells like the Solway, but ebbs like its tide—
And now am I come, with this lost love of mine,
To lead but one measure, drink one cup of wine.
There are maidens in Scotland more lovely by far,
That would gladly be bride to the young Lochinvar."

The bride kissed the goblet: the knight took it up,
He quaffed off the wine, and he threw down the cup.
She looked down to blush, and she looked up to sigh,
With a smile on her lips, and a tear in her eye.
He took her soft hand, ere her mother could bar,—
"Now tread we a measure!" said the young Lochinvar.

So stately his form and so lovely her face,
That never a hall such a galliard did grace;
While her mother did fret, and her father did fume,
And the bridegroom stood dangling his bonnet and plume;
And the bride-maidens whispered, "'Twere better by far,
To have matched our fair cousin with young Lochinvar."

One touch to her hand, and one word in her ear,
When they reached the hall-door, and the charger stood near;
So light to the croup the fair lady he swung,
So light to the saddle before her he sprung!
"She is won! we are gone, over bank, bush, and scaur;
They'll have fleet steeds that follow," quoth young Lochinvar.

There was mounting 'mong Graemes of the Netherby clan;
Forsters, Fenwicks, and Musgraves, they rode and they ran:
There was racing and chasing on Cannobie Lee,
But the lost bride of Netherby n'er did they see.
So daring in love, and so dauntless in war,
Have ye e'er heard of gallant like young Lochinvar?

Sir Walter Scott

A New Courtly Sonnet of the Lady Greensleeves

Alas, my Love! ye do me wrong
To cast me off discourteously;
And I have loved you so long,
Delighting in your company.
    Greensleeves was all my joy,
    Greensleeves was my delight;
    Greensleeves was my heart of gold,
    And who but my Lady Greensleeves.

I have been ready at your hand,
To grant whatever you would crave;
I have both waged life and land,
Your love and goodwill for to have.

I bought thee kerchers to thy head,
That were wrought fine and gallantly;
I kept thee both at board and bed,
Which cost my purse well favouredly.

I bought thee petticoats of the best,
The cloth so fine as fine might be;
I gave thee jewels for thy chest,
And all this cost I spent on thee.

Thy purse and eke thy gay gild knives,
Thy pincase gallant to the eye;
No better wore the burgess wives,
And yet thou wouldst not love me.

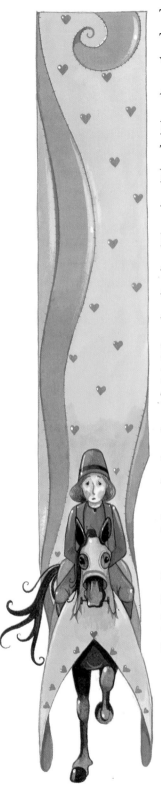

Thy gown was of the grassy green,
Thy sleeves of satin hanging by,
Which made thee be our harvest queen,
And yet thou wouldst not love me.

My gayest gelding I thee gave,
To ride wherever liked thee;
No lady ever was so brave,
And yet thou wouldst not love me.

My men were clothed all in green,
And they did ever wait on thee;
All this was gallant to be seen,
And yet thou wouldst not love me.

For every morning when thou rose,
I sent thee dainties orderly,
To cheer thy stomach from all woes,
And yet thou wouldst not love me.

Well, I will pray to God on high,
That thou my constancy mayst see,
And that yet once before I die,
Thou wilt vouchsafe to love me.

Greensleeves, now farewell! adieu!
God I pray to prosper thee;
For I am still thy lover true.
Come once again and love me.
    Greensleeves was all my joy, etc.

Anonymous,
but some say
King Henry VIII

105

The Night Has a Thousand Eyes

The night has a thousand eyes,
    And the day but one;
Yet the light of the bright world dies
    With the dying sun.

The mind has a thousand eyes,
    And the heart but one;
Yet the light of a whole life dies
    When love is done.

Francis William Bourdillon

Songs
and
Ballads

Thomas the Rhymer

True Thomas lay o'er yond grassy bank,
    And he beheld a ladie gay,
A ladie that was brisk and bold,
    Come riding o'er the fernie brae.

Her skirt was of the grass-green silk,
    Her mantel of the velvet fine,
At ilka tett of her horse's mane
    Hung fifty silver bells and nine.

True Thomas he took off his hat,
    And bowed him low down till his knee:
All hail, thou mighty Queen of Heaven!
    For your peer on earth I never did see.

O no, O no, True Thomas, she says,
    That name does not belong to me;
I am but the queen of fair Elfland,
    And I'm come here for to visit thee.

But ye maun go wi' me now, Thomas,
    True Thomas, ye maun go wi' me,
For ye maun serve me seven years,
    Thro weel or wae as may chance to be.

She turned about her milk-white steed,
    And took True Thomas up behind,
And aye whene'er her bridle rang,
    The steed flew swifter than the wind.

O they rade on, and further on,
    Until they came to a garden green:
Light down, light down, ye ladie free,
    Some of that fruit let me pull to thee.

O no, O no, True Thomas, she says,
    That fruit maun not be touched by thee,
For a' the plagues that are in hell
    Light on the fruit of this countrie.

But I have a loaf here in my lap,
    Likewise a bottle of claret wine,
And now ere we go farther on,
    We'll rest a while, and ye may dine.

When he had eaten and drunk his fill,
    Lay down your head upon my knee,
The lady sayd, ere we climb yon hill,
    And I will show you fairlies three.

O see not ye yon narrow road,
    So thick beset wi' thorns and briers?
That is the path of righteousness,
    Tho after it but few enquires.

And see not ye that braid braid road,
    That lies across yon lillie leven?
That is the path of wickedness,
    Tho some call it the road to heaven.

And see not ye that bonny road,
    Which winds about the fernie brae?
That is the road to fair Elfland,
    Where you and I this night maun gae.

But Thomas, ye maun hold your tongue,
    Whatever you may hear or see,
For gin ae word you should chance to speak,
    You will ne'er get back to your ain countrie.

For forty days and forty nights
    He wade thro red blude to the knee,
And he saw neither sun nor moon,
    But heard the roaring of the sea.

He has gotten a coat of the even cloth,
    And a pair of shoes of velvet green,
And till seven years were past and gone
    True Thomas on earth was never seen.

Anonymous

Bonny Barbara Allan

It was in and about the Martinmas time,
    When the green leaves were a-falling,
That Sir John Graeme in the West Country
    Fell in love with Barbara Allan.

He sent his man down through the town,
    To the place where she was dwelling,
O haste, and come to my master dear,
    Gin ye be Barbara Allan.

O hooly, hooly rose she up,
    To the place where he was lying,
And when she drew the curtain by,
    Young man, I think you're dying.

O it's I'm sick, and very very sick,
    And 'tis a' for Barbara Allan,
O the better for me ye's never be,
    Tho your heart's blood were a-spilling.

O dinna ye mind, young man, said she,
    When ye was in the tavern a-drinking,
That ye made the healths gae round and round,
    And slighted Barbara Allan?

He turned his face unto the wall,
    And death was with him dealing;
Adieu, adieu, my dear friends all,
    And be kind to Barbara Allan.

And slowly, slowly raise she up,
    And slowly, slowly left him;
And sighing, said, she could not stay,
    Since death of life had reft him.

She had not gane a mile but twa,
    When she heard the dead-bell ringing,
And every jow that the dead-bell gied,
    It cry'd, Woe to Barbara Allan.

O mother, mother, make my bed,
    O make it saft and narrow,
Since my love died for me today,
    I'll die for him tomorrow.

Anonymous

The Great Silkie of Sule Skerrie

An earthly nourris sits and sings,
    And aye she sings, Ba, lily wean!
Little ken I my bairn's father,
    Far less the land that he staps in.

Then ane arose at her bed-fit,
    An' a grumly guest I'm sure was he:
Here am I, thy bairn's father,
    Although that I be not comelie.

I am a man, upon the land,
    An' I am a silkie in the sea,
And when I'm far and far frae land,
    My dwelling is in Sule Skerry.

114

It was na weel, quo' the maiden fair,
    It was na weel, indeed, quo' she,
That the Great Silkie of Sule Skerry
    Should hae come and aught a bairn to me.

Now he has ta'en a purse of goud,
    And he has put it upo' her knee,
Sayin', Gie to me my little young son,
    An' tak thee up they nourrice-fee.

An' it sall pass on a summer's day,
    When the sun shines het on evera stane,
That I will tak my little young son,
    An' teach him for to swim the faem.

An' thu sall marry a proud gunner,
    An' a proud gunner I'm sure he'll be,
An' the very first shot that ere he shoots,
    He'll shoot baith my young son and me.

Anonymous

The Yarn of the Nancy Bell

'Twas on the shores that round our coast
    From Deal to Ramsgate span,
That I found alone on a piece of stone
    An elderly naval man.

His hair was weedy, his beard was long,
    And weedy and long was he,
And I heard this wight on the shore recite,
    In a singular minor key:

"Oh, I am a cook and a captain bold,
    And the mate of the *Nancy* brig,
And a bo'sun tight, and a midshipmite,
    And the crew of the captain's gig."

And he shook his fists and he tore his hair,
    Till I really felt afraid,
For I couldn't help thinking the man had been drinking,
    And so I simply said:

"Oh, elderly man, it's little I know
    Of the duties of men of the sea,
And I'll eat my hand if I understand
    How you can possibly be

"At once a cook, and a captain bold,
    And the mate of the *Nancy* brig,
And a bo'sun tight, and a midshipmite,
    And the crew of the captain's gig."

Then he gave a hitch to his trousers, which
 Is a trick all seamen larn,
And having got rid of a thumping quid,
 He spun this painful yarn:

"'Twas in the good ship *Nancy Bell*
 That we sailed to the Indian sea
And there on a reef we come to grief,
 Which has often occurred to me.

"And pretty nigh all o' the crew was drowned
 (There was seventy-seven o' soul),
And only ten of the *Nancy's* men
 Said 'Here!' to the muster-roll.

"There was me and the cook and the captain bold,
 And the mate of the *Nancy* brig,
And a bo'sun tight, and a midshipmite,
 And the crew of the captain's gig.

"For a month we'd neither wittles nor drink,
 Till a-hungry we did feel,
So we drawed a lot, and accordin' shot
 The captain for our meal.

"The next lot fell to the *Nancy's* mate,
    And a delicate dish he made;
Then our appetite with the midshipmite
    We seven survivors stayed.

"And then we murdered the bo'sun tight,
    And he much resembled pig;
Then we wittled free, did the cook and me,
    On the crew of the captain's gig.

"Then only the cook and me was left,
    And the delicate question, 'Which
Of us two goes to the kettle?' arose,
    And we argued it out as sich.

"For I loved that cook as a brother, I did,
    And the cook he worshipped me;
But we'd both be blowed if we'd either be stowed
    In the other chap's hold, you see.

"'I'll be eat if you dines off me,' says Tom,
    'Yes, that,' says I, 'you'll be,'—
'I'm boiled if I die, my friend,' quoth I,
    And 'Exactly so,' quoth he.

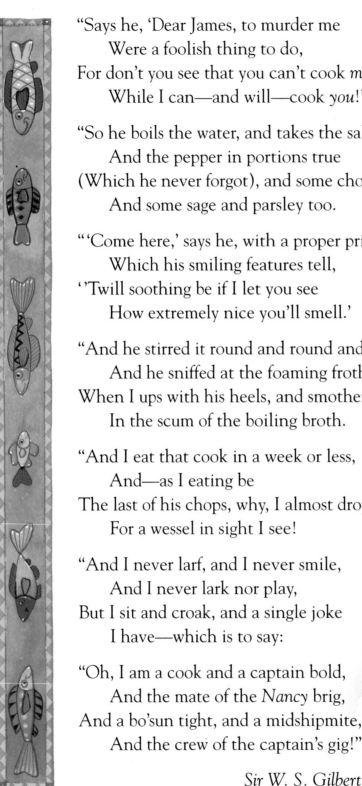

"Says he, 'Dear James, to murder me
    Were a foolish thing to do,
For don't you see that you can't cook *me*,
    While I can—and will—cook *you*!'

"So he boils the water, and takes the salt
    And the pepper in portions true
(Which he never forgot), and some chopped shallot,
    And some sage and parsley too.

"'Come here,' says he, with a proper pride,
    Which his smiling features tell,
''Twill soothing be if I let you see
    How extremely nice you'll smell.'

"And he stirred it round and round and round,
    And he sniffed at the foaming froth;
When I ups with his heels, and smothers his squeals
    In the scum of the boiling broth.

"And I eat that cook in a week or less,
    And—as I eating be
The last of his chops, why, I almost drops,
    For a wessel in sight I see!

"And I never larf, and I never smile,
    And I never lark nor play,
But I sit and croak, and a single joke
    I have—which is to say:

"Oh, I am a cook and a captain bold,
    And the mate of the *Nancy* brig,
And a bo'sun tight, and a midshipmite,
    And the crew of the captain's gig!"

Sir W. S. Gilbert

120

BOYS
and
GIRLS

What Am I After All

What am I after all but a child, pleas'd with the sound of
    my own name? repeating it over and over;
I stand apart to hear—it never tires me.

To you your name also;
Did you think there was nothing but two or three
    pronunciations in the sound of your name?

Walt Whitman

Jemima

There was a little girl, and she wore a little curl
    Right down the middle of her forehead,
When she was good, she was very, very, good,
    But when she was bad, she was horrid!

One day she went upstairs, while her parents, unawares,
    In the kitchen down below were occupied with meals,
And she stood upon her head, on her little truckle bed,
    And she then began hurraying with her heels.

Her mother heard the noise, and thought it was the boys
    A-playing at a combat in the attic,
But when she climbed the stair and saw Jemima there,
    She took and she did whip her most emphatic.

Anonymous

There Was a Naughty Boy

There was a naughty Boy
   A naughty Boy was he
He would not stop at home
He could not quiet be—
   He took
   In his Knapsack
   A Book
   Full of vowels
   And a shirt
   With some towels—
   A slight cap
   For night cap—
   A hair brush
   Comb ditto
   New Stockings
   For old ones
   Would split O!
   This Knapsack
   Tight at's back
   He rivetted close
And follow'd his Nose
   To the North
   To the North
And follow'd his Nose
   To the North.

There was a naughty Boy
    And a naughty Boy was he
He ran away to Scotland
    The people for to see—
        There he found
        That the ground
        Was as hard
        That a yard
        Was as long,
        That a song
        Was as merry,
        That a cherry
        Was as red—
        That lead
        Was as weighty
        That forescore
        Was as eighty
        That a door
        Was as wooden
        As in England—
        So he stood in
        His shoes
        And he wonder'd
        He stood in his
        Shoes and he wonder'd.

John Keats

The False Knight and the Wee Boy

"O whare are ye gaun?"
    Quo' the fause knicht upon the road:
"I'm gaun to the scule,"
    Quo' the wee boy, and still he stude.

"What is that upon your back?"
    Quo' the fause knicht upon the road:
"Atweel it is my bukes,"
    Quo' the wee boy, and still he stude.

"Wha's aucht thae sheep?"
    Quo' the fause knicht upon the road:
"They are mine and my mither's,"
    Quo' the wee boy, and still he stude.

"How mony o' them are mine?"
    Quo' the fause knicht upon the road:
"A' they that hae blue tails,"
    Quo' the wee boy, and still he stude.

"I wiss ye were on yon tree,"
    Quo' the fause knicht upon the road:
"And for you to fa' down,"
    Quo' the wee boy, and still he stude.

"I wiss ye were in yon sie,"
    Quo' the fause knicht upon the road:
"And a gude bottom under me,"
    Quo' the wee boy, and still he stude.

126

"And the bottom for to break,"
    Quo' the fause knicht upon the road:
"*And ye to be drowned,*"
    Quo' the wee boy, and still he stude.

Anonymous

127

Children

Come to me, O ye children!
    For I hear you at your play,
And the questions that perplexed me
    Have vanished quite away.

Ye open the eastern windows,
    That look towards the sun,
Where thoughts are singing swallows
    And the brooks of morning run.

In your hearts are the birds and the sunshine,
    In your thoughts the brooklet's flow,
But in mine is the wind of Autumn
    And the first fall of the snow.

Ah! what would the world be to us
    If the children were no more?
We should dread the desert behind us
    Worse than the dark before.

What the leaves are to the forest,
    With light and air for food,
Ere their sweet and tender juices
    Have been hardened into wood,—

That to the world are children;
    Through them it feels the glow
Of a brighter and sunnier climate
    Than reaches the trunks below.

Come to me, O ye children!
And whisper in my ear
What the birds and the winds are singing
   In your sunny atmosphere.

For what are all our contrivings,
   And the wisdom of our books,
What compared with your caresses,
   And the gladness of your looks?

Ye are better than all the ballads
   That ever were sung or said;
For ye are living poems,
   And all the rest are dead.

Henry Wadsworth Longfellow

When That I Was and a Little Tiny Boy

When that I was and a little tiny boy,
    With hey, ho, the wind and the rain;
A foolish thing was but a toy,
    For the rain it raineth every day.

For when I came to man's estate,
    With hey, ho, the wind and the rain;
'Gainst knaves and thieves men shut their gate,
    For the rain it raineth every day.

But when I came, alas! to wive,
    With hey, ho, the wind and the rain;
By swaggering could I never thrive,
    For the rain it raineth every day.

But when I came unto my beds,
    With hey, ho, the wind and the rain;
With toss-pots still had drunken heads,
    For the rain it raineth every day.

A great while ago the world begun,
    With hey, ho, the wind and the rain;
But that's all one, our play is done,
    And we'll strive to please you every day.

William Shakespeare

130

MAGIC
and
MYSTERY

Waltzing Matilda

Once a jolly swagman camped by a billabong,
    Under the shade of a coolabah tree;
And he sang as he watched and waited till his billy boiled,
    "You'll come a-waltzing Matilda with me!"

"Waltzing Matilda, Waltzing Matilda,
    You'll come a-waltzing Matilda with me,"
And he sang as he watched and waited till his billy boiled,
    "You'll come a-waltzing Matilda with me."

Down came a jumbuck to drink at the billabong,
    Up jumped the swagman and grabbed him with glee;
And he sang as he shoved that jumbuck in his tucker-bag,
    "You'll come a-waltzing Matilda with me."

"Waltzing Matilda, Waltzing Matilda,
    You'll come a-waltzing Matilda with me,"
And he sang as he shoved that jumbuck in his tucker-bag,
    "You'll come a-waltzing Matilda with me."

Up rode the squatter mounted on his thoroughbred;
    Down came the troopers—one, two and three.
"Whose the jolly jumbuck you've got in your tucker-bag?
    You'll come a-waltzing Matilda with me."

"Waltzing Matilda, Waltzing Matilda,
    You'll come a-waltzing Matilda with me,
Whose the jolly jumbuck you've got in your tucker-bag?
    You'll come a-waltzing Matilda with me."

Up jumped the swagman, sprang into the billabong,
    "You'll never catch me alive," said he.
And his ghost may be heard as you pass by that billabong,
    "Who'll come a-waltzing Matilda with me?"

"Waltzing Matilda, Waltzing Matilda,
    You'll come a-waltzing Matilda with me,"
And his ghost may be heard as you pass by that billabong,
    "Who'll come a-waltzing Matilda with me?"

A. B. Paterson

The Ghost's Song

Wae's me! wae's me!
The acorn's not yet
Fallen from the tree
That's to grow the wood,
That's to make the cradle,
That's to rock the bairn,
That's to grow a man,
That's to lay me.

Anonymous

133

John Barleycorn

There was three Kings into the east,
    Three Kings both great and high,
And they hae sworn a solemn oath
    John Barleycorn should die.

They took a plough and plough'd him down,
    Put clods upon his head,
And they hae sworn a solemn oath
    John Barleycorn was dead.

But the cheerfu' Spring came kindly on,
    And show'rs began to fall;
John Barleycorn got up again,
    And sore surprised them all.

The sultry suns of Summer came,
    And he grew thick and strong,
His head weel arm'd wi' pointed spears,
    That no one should him wrong.

The sober Autumn enter'd mild,
    When he grew wan and pale;
His bending joints and drooping head
    Show'd he began to fail.

His colour sicken'd more and more,
    He faded into age;
And then his enemies began
    To shew their deadly rage.

They've ta'en a weapon, long and sharp,
    And cut him by the knee;
Then tied him fast upon a cart,
    Like a rogue for forgerie.

They laid him down upon his back,
    And cudgell'd him full sore;
They hung him up before the storm,
    And turn'd him o'er and o'er.

They filled up a darksome pit
    With water to the brim,
They heaved in John Barleycorn,
    There let him sink or swim.

They laid him out upon the floor,
    To work him farther woe,
And still, as signs of life appear'd,
    They toss'd him to and fro.

They wasted, o'er a scorching flame,
    The marrow of his bones;
But a miller us'd him worst of all,
    For he crush'd him between two stones.

And they hae ta'en his very heart's blood,
    And drank it round and round;
And still the more and more they drank,
    Their joy did more abound.

John Barleycorn was a hero bold,
    Of noble enterprise,
For if you do but taste his blood,
    'Twill make your courage rise;

'Twill make a man forget his woe;
    'Twill heighten all his joy:
'Twill make the widow's heart to sing,
    Tho' the tear were in her eye.

Then let us toast John Barleycorn,
    Each man a glass in hand;
And may his great posterity
    Ne'er fail in old Scotland!

Robert Burns

A Strange Visitor

A wife was sitting at her reel ae night;
And aye she sat, and aye she reeled, and aye she wished for company.

In came a pair o' braid braid soles, and sat down at the fireside;
And aye she sat, and aye she reeled, and aye she wished for company.

In came a pair o' sma' sma' legs, and sat down on the braid braid soles;
And aye she sat, and aye she reeled, and aye she wished for company.

In came a pair o' muckle muckle knees, and sat down on the sma' sma' legs;
And aye she sat, and aye she reeled, and aye she wished for company.

In came a pair o' sma' sma' thees, and sat down on the muckle muckle knees;
And aye she sat, and aye she reeled, and aye she wished for company.

In came a pair o' muckle muckle hips, and sat down on the sma' sma' thees;
And aye she sat, and aye she reeled, and aye she wished for company.

In came a sma' sma' waist, and sat down on the muckle muckle hips;
And aye she sat, and aye she reeled, and aye she wished for company.

In came a pair o' braid braid shouthers, and sat down on the sma' sma' waist;
And aye she sat, and aye she reeled, and aye she wished for company.

In came a pair o' sma' sma' arms, and sat down on the braid braid shouthers;
And aye she sat, and aye she reeled, and aye she wished for company.

In came a pair o' muckle muckle hands, and sat down on the sma' sma' arms;
And aye she sat, and aye she reeled, and aye she wished for company.

In came a sma' sma' neck, and sat down on the braid braid shouthers;
And aye she sat, and aye she reeled, and aye she wished for company.

In came a great big head, and sat down on the sma' sma' neck;
And aye she sat, and aye she reeled, and aye she wished for company.

"What way hae ye sic braid braid feet?" quo' the wife.
"Muckle ganging, muckle ganging."
"What way hae ye sic sma' sma' legs?"
"*Aih-h-h!*—late—and *wee-e-e* moul."
"What way hae ye sic muckle muckle knees?"
"Muckle praying, muckle praying."
"What way hae ye sic sma' sma' thees?"
"*Aih-h-h!*—late—and *wee-e-e* moul."
"What way hae ye sic big big hips?"
"Muckle sitting, muckle sitting."
"What way hae ye sic a sma' sma' waist?"
"*Aih-h-h!*—late—and *wee-e-e* moul."
"What way hae ye sic braid braid shouthers?"
"Wi' carying broom, wi' carying broom."
"What way hae ye sic sma' sma' arms?"
"*Aih-h-h!*—late—and *wee-e-e* moul."
"What way hae ye sic muckle muckle hands?"
"Threshing wi' an iron flail, threshing wi' an iron flail."
"What way hae ye sic a sma' sma' neck?"
"*Aih-h-h!*—late—and *wee-e-e* moul."
"What way hae ye sic a muckle muckle head?"
"Muckle wit, muckle wit."
"What do you come for?"
"For YOU!"

Anonymous

The Oxen

Christmas Eve, and twelve of the clock.
  "Now they are all on their knees,"
An elder said as we sat in a flock
  By the embers in hearthside ease.

We pictured the meek mild creatures where
  They dwelt in their strawy pen,
Nor did it occur to one of us there
  To doubt they were kneeling then.

So fair a fancy few would weave
  In these years! Yet, I feel,
If someone said on Christmas Eve,
  "Come; see the oxen kneel,

"In the lonely barton by yonder coomb
  Our childhood used to know,"
I should go with him in the gloom,
  Hoping it might be so.

Thomas Hardy

SIGHTS
and
SOUNDS

Upon Westminster Bridge

Earth has nothing to show more fair:
Dull would he be of soul who could pass by
A sight so touching in its majesty:
This City now doth, like a garment, wear
The beauty of the morning; silent, bare,
Ships, towers, domes, theatres, and temples lie
Open unto the fields, and to the sky;
All bright and glittering in the smokeless air.
Never did sun more beautifully steep
In his first splendour, valley, rock, or hill;
Ne'er saw I, never felt, a calm so deep!
The river glideth at his own sweet will:
Dear God! the very houses seem asleep;
And all that mighty heart is lying still!

William Wordsworth

On First Looking into Chapman's Homer

Much have I travell'd in the realms of gold,
    And many goodly states and kingdoms seen;
    Round many western islands have I been
Which bards in fealty to Apollo hold.
    That deep-brow'd Homer ruled as his demesne;
    Yet did I never breathe its pure serene
Till I heard Chapman speak out loud and bold:
Then felt I like some watcher of the skies
    When a new planet swims into his ken;
Or like stout Cortez when with eagle eyes
    He star'd at the Pacific—and all his men
Look'd at each other with a wild surmise—
    Silent, upon a peak in Darien.

John Keats

143

Symphony in Yellow

An omnibus across the bridge
Crawls like a yellow butterfly,
And, here and there, a passer-by
Shows like a little restless midge.

Big barges full of yellow hay
Are moored against the shadowy wharf,
And, like a yellow silken scarf,
The thick fog hangs along the quay.

The yellow leaves begin to fade
And flutter from the Temple elms,
And at my feet the pale green Thames
Lies like a rod of rippled jade.

Oscar Wilde

144

A Thing of Beauty

A thing of beauty is a joy for ever:
Its loveliness increases; it will never
Pass into nothingness; but still will keep
A bower quiet for us, and a sleep
Full of sweet dreams, and health, and quiet breathing.
Therefore, on every morrow, are we wreathing
A flowery band to bind us to the earth,
Spite of despondence, of the inhuman death
Of noble natures, of the gloomy days,
Of all the unhealthy and o'er-darkened ways
Made for our searching: yes, in spite of all,
Some shape of beauty moves away the pall
From our dark spirits.

John Keats

145

From *The Garden*

What wondrous life in this I lead!
Ripe apples drop about my head;
The luscious clusters of the vine
Upon my mouth do crush their wine;
The nectarine, and curious peach,
Into my hands themselves do reach;
Stumbling on melons, as I pass,
Ensnared with flowers, I fall on grass.

Meanwhile the mind, from pleasure less,
Withdraws into its happiness:
The mind, that ocean where each kind
Does straight its own resemblance find;
Yet it creates, transcending these,
Far other worlds, and other seas;
Annihilating all that's made
To a green thought in a green shade.

Andrew Marvell

MUSIC
and
DANCING

Song's Eternity

What is song's eternity?
    Come and see.
Can it noise and bustle be?
    Come and see.
Praises sung or praises said
    Can it be?
Wait awhile and these are dead—
    Sigh—sigh;
Be they high or lowly bred
    They die.

What is song's eternity?
    Come and see.
Melodies of earth and sky,
    Here they be.
Song once sung to Adam's ears
    Can it be?
Ballads of six thousand years
    Thrive, thrive;
Songs awaken with the spheres
    Alive.

Mighty songs that miss decay,
    What are they?
Crowds and cities pass away
    Like a day.
Books are out and books are read;
    What are they?
Years will lay them with the dead—
    Sigh, sigh;
Trifles unto nothing wed,
    They die.

Dreamers, mark the honey bee;
    Mark the tree
Where the blue cap "*tootle tee*"
    Sings a glee
Sung to Adam and to Eve—
    Here they be.
When floods covered every bough,
    Noah's ark
Heard that ballad singing now;
    Hark, hark,

"*Tootle tootle tootle tee*"—
    Can it be
Pride and fame must shadows be?
    Come and see—
Every season own her own;
    Bird and bee
Sing creation's music on;
    Nature's glee
Is in every mood and tone
    Eternity.

John Clare

Music

Orpheus with his lute made trees,
 And the mountain-tops that freeze,
Bow themselves when he did sing.
 To his music plants and flowers
Ever sprung: as sun and showers
 There had made a lasting spring.
Everything that heard him play,
 Even the billows of the sea,
Hung their heads, and then lay by.
 In sweet music is such art,
Killing care and grief of heart
 Fall asleep, or, hearing, die.

John Fletcher

Piano

Softly, in the dusk, a woman is singing to me;
Taking me back down the vista of years, till I see
A child sitting under the piano, in the boom of the tingling strings
And pressing the small, poised feet of a mother who smiles as she sings.

In spite of myself, the insidious mastery of song
Betrays me back, till the heart of me weeps to belong
To the old Sunday evenings at home, with winter outside
And hymns in the cosy parlour, the tinkling piano our guide.

So now it is vain for the singer to burst into clamour
With the great black piano appassionato. The glamour
Of childish days is upon me, my manhood is cast
Down in the flood of remembrance, I weep like a child for the past.

D. H. Lawrence

I Am of Ireland

I am of Ireland,
And of the holy land
Of Ireland.

Good sir, pray I thee,
For of saint charity,
Come and dance with me
In Ireland.

Anonymous

To Emilia V—

Music, when soft voices die,
Vibrates in the memory—
Odours, when sweet violets sicken,
Live within the sense they quicken.

Rose leaves, when the rose is dead,
Are heaped for the beloved's bed—
And so thy thoughts, when thou art gone,
Love itself shall slumber on…

Percy Bysshe Shelley

152

SADNESS
and
HAPPINESS

So, We'll Go No More A-Roving

So, we'll go no more a-roving
    So late into the night,
Though the heart be still as loving,
    And the moon be still as bright.

For the sword outwears its sheath,
    And the soul wears out the breast,
And the heart must pause to breathe,
    And love itself have rest.

Though the night was made for loving,
    And the day returns too soon,
Yet we'll go no more a-roving
    By the light of the moon.

George Gordon, Lord Byron

Spring and Fall

to a young child

Margaret, are you grieving
Over Goldengrove unleaving?
Leaves, like the things of man, you
With your fresh thoughts care for, can you?
Ah! as the heart grows older
It will come to such sights colder
By and by, nor spare a sigh
Though worlds of wanwood leafmeal lie,
And yet you *will* weep and know why.
Now no matter, child, the name:
Sorrow's springs are the same.
Nor mouth had, no nor mind, expressed
What heart heard of, ghost guessed:
It is the blight man was born for,
It is Margaret you mourn for.

Gerard Manley Hopkins

Canadian Boat Song

Listen to me, as when ye heard our father
Sing long ago the song of other shores—
Listen to me, and then in chorus gather
All your deep voices as ye pull your oars:
    Fair these broad meads—these hoary woods are grand
    But we are exiles from our fathers' land.

From the lone shieling of the misty island
Mountains divide us, and the waste of seas,
Yet still the blood is strong, the heart is Highland,
And we in dreams behold the Hebrides.

We ne'er shall tread the fancy-haunted valley,
Where 'tween the dark hills creeps the small clear stream,
In arms around the patriarch banner rally,
Nor see the moon on royal tombstones gleam.

When the bold kindred in the time long vanished,
Conquered the soil and fortified the keep—
No seer foretold the children would be banished,
That a degenerate lord might boast his sheep.

Come foreign rage—let Discord burst in slaughter!
O then for clansmen true, and stern claymore,
The hearts that would have given their blood like water,
Beat heavily beyond the Atlantic roar.
    Fair these broad meads—these hoary woods are grand
    But we are exiles from our fathers' land.

Anonymous

156

In the Highlands

In the highlands, in the country places,
Where the old plain men have rosy faces,
And the young fair maidens
Quiet eyes;
Where essential silence cheers and blesses,
And for ever in the hill-recesses
Her more lovely music
Broods and dies.

O to mount again where erst I haunted;
Where the old red hills are bird-enchanted,
And the low green meadows
Bright with sward;
And when even dies, the million-tinted,
And the night has come, and planets glinted,
Lo, the valley hollow
Lamp-bestarred!

O to dream, O to awake and wander
There, and with delight to take and render,
Through the trance of silence,
Quiet breath;
Lo! for there, among the flowers and grasses,
Only the mightier movement sounds and passes;
Only winds and rivers,
Life and death.

Robert Louis Stevenson

When in Disgrace With Fortune

When in disgrace with Fortune and men's eyes
I all alone beweep my outcast state,
And trouble deaf heaven with my bootless cries,
And look upon myself and curse my fate,
Wishing me like to one more rich in hope,
Featured like him, like him with friends possessed,
Desiring this man's art, and that man's scope,
With what I most enjoy contented least,
Yet in these thoughts myself almost despising,
Haply I think on thee, and then my state
(Like to the lark at break of day arising
From sullen earth) sings hymns at heaven's gate,
  For thy sweet love remembered such wealth brings,
  That then I scorn to change my state with kings.

William Shakespeare

Piping Down the Valleys Wild

Piping down the valleys wild,
Piping songs of pleasant glee,
On a cloud I saw a child,
And he laughing said to me:

"Pipe a song about a Lamb!"
So I piped with merry chear.
"Piper, pipe that song again;"
So I piped: he wept to hear.

"Drop thy pipe, thy happy pipe;
"Sing thy songs of happy chear:"
So I sung the same again,
While he wept with joy to hear.

"Piper, sit thee down and write
In a book, that all may read."
So he vanish'd from my sight,
And I pluck'd a hollow reed,

And I made a rural pen,
And I stain'd the water clear,
And I wrote my happy songs
Every child may joy to hear.

William Blake

A Lark's Nest

Now's the time for mirth and play,
Saturday's an holiday;
Praise to heav'n unceasing yield,
I've found a lark's nest in the field.

A lark's nest, then your play-mate begs
You'd spare herself and speckled eggs;
Soon she shall ascend and sing
Your praise to th'eternal King.

Christopher Smart

From *The Song of Solomon*

My beloved spake, and said unto me, Rise up, my love, my fair one, and
come away.
For lo, the winter is past, the rain is over, and gone.
The flowers appear on the earth, the time of the singing of birds is come,
and the voice of the turtle is heard in our land.
The fig tree putteth forth her green figs, and the vines with the tender
grape give a good smell.
Arise, my love, my fair one, and come away.

King James Bible

The Swing

How do you like to go up in a swing,
Up in the air so blue?
Oh, I do think it the pleasantest thing
Ever a child can do!

Up in the air and over the wall
Till I can see so wide,
Rivers and trees and cattle and all
Over the countryside—

Till I look down on the garden green,
Down on the roof so brown—
Up in the air I go flying again,
Up in the air and down!

Robert Louis Stevenson

Requiem

Under the wide and starry sky,
Dig the grave and let me lie.
Glad did I live and gladly die,
And I laid me down with a will.

This be the verse you grave for me:
Here he lies where he longed to be;
Home is the sailor, home from the sea,
And the hunter home from the hill.

Robert Louis Stevenson

ABOUT THE POETS

WILLIAM ALLINGHAM
1824–89
Pages 50, 82 This Irish poet wrote many volumes of poetry, including some based on traditional Irish myths and legends.

WILLIAM BLAKE
1757–1827
Pages 16, 24, 33, 42, 160 Born in London, Blake was a painter and engraver as well as a poet. He illustrated many of his own poems with vivid engravings.

FRANCIS WILLIAM BOURDILLON
1852–1921
Page 106 Bourdillon was an English poet. This is his best known work. The first line is based on a line by the sixteenth-century poet Lyly.

EMILY BRONTE
1818–48
Page 35 One of the three famous Brontë sisters, Emily is best known for her only novel, *Wuthering Heights*, which she published under the name of Ellis Bell.

ROBERT BROWNING
1812–89
Page 36, 64 Browning's poems attracted much attention during his lifetime, including that of fellow poet Elizabeth Barrett.
They were married in 1846.

ROBERT BURNS
1759–96
Page 100, 134 This Scottish poet was very famous during his lifetime for his poems and songs. He worked on a farm in his early years and later, when his writing had brought him wealth, bought his own farm.

GEORGE GORDON, LORD BYRON
1788–1824
Page 44, 154 A romantic figure, very popular during his lifetime, Byron died of fever in Greece, supporting a Greek uprising.

LEWIS CARROLL
1832–98
Page 14, 18 Lewis Carroll's real name was Charles Dodgson. He became famous for his children's books, *Alice's Adventures in Wonderland* and *Through the Looking Glass*.

JOHN CLARE
1794–1864

Page 148 Although he had little education, John Clare wrote movingly about the countryside and his feelings of loss and sadness. His life was difficult and often unhappy, but his poems still move us today.

ARTHUR HUGH CLOUGH
1819–61

Page 67 Clough's father emigrated to the U.S.A. His son returned to England to live and work, but had many American friends.

SAMUEL TAYLOR COLERIDGE
1772–1834

Page 48 A poet and thinker, Coleridge was a great friend of the poet William Wordsworth.

EMILY DICKINSON
1830–86

Page 58 This American poet lived a secluded life in Massachussets, writing over a thousand poems. Their original forms and use of language have influenced many modern poets.

EUGENE FIELD
1850–95

Page 90 This American journalist is now famous for his poems for children.

JOHN FLETCHER
1579–1625

Page 150 Known mainly as a playwright, Fletcher was writing in London at the same time as Shakespeare and may have worked with him on some plays.

SIR W. S. GILBERT
1836–1911

Page 116 Gilbert is best known for his writing the words in the famous musical partnership with Sir Arthur Sullivan.

THOMAS HARDY
1840–1928

Page 140 This poet and novelist was born in the south-west of England, which appears over and over again in his work.

ROBERT HERRICK
1591–1674

Page 79 This English poet wrote chiefly of love, youth and figures from ancient Greece and Rome.

THOMAS HOOD
1799–1845
Page 80 Born in London, this poet and humourist contributed to many popular magazines.

GERARD MANLEY HOPKINS
1844–89
Page 38, 155 As a young man, Hopkins became a Roman Catholic; many of his poems have a religious theme.

ROBERT JONES
lived around 1600
Page 98 Jones wrote songs for several voices, called madrigals, and simpler airs, such as *Robin Hood*, to be sung to the lute, a stringed instrument.

JOHN KEATS
1795–1821
Pages 30, 52, 124, 143, 145 Trained as a doctor, Keats wrote many wonderful poems before dying, still a very young man, in Rome, Italy.

D. H. LAWRENCE
1885–1930
Page 151 The son of a miner, Lawrence wrote several novels set in the mining area of the English Midlands, as well as others reflecting his many travels abroad.

EDWARD LEAR
1812–88
Page 12 An artist and author, Lear wrote many serious books but is best known for his *Book of Nonsense*, published in 1846.

HENRY WADSWORTH
LONGFELLOW 1807–82
Pages 34, 128 As well as short poems, Longfellow enjoyed telling long stories in verse, such as *Hiawatha*.

ANDREW MARVELL
1621–78
Page 146 Marvell spent the early part of his working life as a tutor to wealthy families. Later, he became an energetic politician and a defender of the poet John Milton.

HERMAN MELVILLE
1819–91
Page 19 Born in New York, Melville is perhaps most famous for his sea-faring novel, *Moby Dick*.

A. B. PATERSON
1864–1941
Page 132 The famous Australian poem *Waltzing Matilda* has been attributed to this poet, although some people think it was based on an older ballad.

EDGAR ALLAN POE
1809–49
Page 68 This American poet and story-teller particularly enjoyed mysterious and spine-chilling subjects.

JAMES WHITCOMB RILEY
1849–1916
Page 76 This American poet was born in Indiana. *Little Orfant Annie* is his most famous poem.

CHRISTINA ROSSETTI
1830–94
Pages 16, 27, 28, 57, 71, 89, 101 The poet's Italian father settled in London before her birth. She also has a famous brother, the painter and poet Dante Gabriel Rossetti.

SIR WALTER SCOTT
1771–1832
Pages 19, 102 A poet and a novelist, Scott celebrated all things Scottish in his work.

WILLIAM SHAKESPEARE
1564–1616
Pages 32, 45, 56, 130, 159 Perhaps the greatest playwright in the English language, Shakespeare lived in the time of Elizabeth I.

PERCY BYSSHE SHELLEY
1792–1822
Pages 66, 152 Shelley shocked English society with his beliefs. His later years were spent abroad.

CHRISTOPHER SMART
1722–71
Pages 20, 161 As well as writing poetry, Smart also made translations of the Bible.

ROBERT LOUIS STEVENSON
1850–94
Pages 29, 40, 54, 70, 72, 74, 84, 86, 88, 158, 162, 163 A popular writer of adventure stories, Stevenson is perhaps best known for his *Treasure Island.*

ALFRED, LORD TENNYSON
1809–92
Pages 22, 23, 46, 62 Tennyson's poems and verse-stories enjoyed huge popularity in his lifetime.

WALT WHITMAN
1819–92
Pages 60, 122 Whitman's varied life and experiences in the American Civil War are reflected in his poetry, but he did not find real fame until after his death.

OSCAR WILDE
1854–1900
Pages 144 Wilde's life ended sadly in France, but his witty and elegant plays are still widely performed today. They include *Lady Windermere's Fan* and *The Importance of Being Ernest.* He also wrote poetry and several stories for children.

WILLIAM WORDSWORTH
1770–1850
Pages 39, 142 Wordsworth is best known as a poet of nature, expressing his love for the Lake District, England.

GLOSSARY

a' all
ae one
ain own
alighted got down from his horse
ane one
atweel know well
aught a bairn to me had a child with me
aye always
bairn child
baith both
barton barn
beweep cry about
billabong dead-end water-filled channel
billy can
blude blood
bootless fruitless
brae brow of a hill
braid broad
brake thicket
bukes books
burgess well-to-do citizen
charger war-horse
chear cheer
claymore broadsword
comelie handsome
coolabah tree kind of gum tree
coomb valley
croup hindquarters (of a horse)
dauntless bold
demesne estate
dinna don't
eke also
ere before
erst first
even evening
fa' fall
faem foam
fairlies wonders

fause false
fealty loyalty, trust
fernie ferny
fleet fast
fleurs-de-lys iris-flower pattern appearing in heraldry
ford river crossing
frae from
galliard courtly dance
gane gone
gang go
ganging going
gaun going
gied gave
gild gilded
gin if
goud gold
grave carve
grumly fierce-looking
gude good
hae have
halcyon calm
haply by chance
het hot
hoary ancient
hooly gently
ilka every
jow stroke
jumbuck sheep
keep strongest part of castle
ken know, knowledge
kerchers kerchiefs, head-dresses
knaves rogues
knicht knight
larn learn
lay (a ghost) put a ghost to rest
lillie leven lovely glade
lily wean lovely little one

mantel cloak
maun must
meads meadows
mither mother
mony many
muckle great
na not
ne'er never
nigh nearly
nourrice, nourris nurse
o' of
o'er over
omnibus horsedrawn bus
pall gloomy covering
putteth puts
quaffed drank
quid piece of tobacco being chewed
quo' said
quoth said
rade rode
reft torn
saft soft
sall shall
scaur cliff
scule school
shew show
shieling hut on grazing land
shouthers shoulders
sic such
sich such
sie sea
silkie seal
sma' thin
spake spoke
squatter sheepstation owner

stane stone
staps steps
steeds horses
stude stood
Sule Skerrie Seal Reef
swagman tramp carrying a swag or bundle
sward grass
ta'en taken
tett lock of hair of mane
thees thighs
thou you
thu you
tucker-bag food bag
turtle turtle dove
twa two
unceasing without stopping
vair fur
wae woe
waged gambled
waltzing Matilda carrying a swag
wan pale
weel well
wessel vessel, ship
wha's aucht thae? whose are those?
whare? where?
what way? why?
wi' with
wight creature
wiss wish
wittles food
wive marry
wrought made
ye you
yon yonder

INDEX OF TITLES AND FIRST LINES

A Birthday	101
About the Shark, phlegmatical one	19
A Child's Grace	79
A Child's Thought	54
A Lark's Nest	161
A New Courtly Sonnet of the Lady	
Greensleeves	104
A Red, Red, Rose	100
A Strange Visitor	137
A Thing of Beauty	145
A thing of beauty is a joy for ever	145
A wife was sitting at her reel ae night	137
At seven, when I go to bed	54
Alas, my Love! ye do me wrong	104
An earthly nourris sits and sings	114
An omnibus across the bridge	144
Auguries of Innocence	16
Bed in Summer	88
Blow, Bugle, Blow	46
Boats sail on the rivers	27
Bonny Barbara Allan	112
Break, Break, Break	62
Break, Break, Break	62
Canadian Boat Song	156
Children	128
Children, you are very little	84
Christmas Eve, and twelve of the	
clock	140
Come to me, O ye children!	128
Daffodils	39
Does the road wind uphill all the way?	71

Earth has nothing to show more fair	142
Eldorado	68
Escape at Bedtime	86
Fall, Leaves, Fall	35
Fall, leaves, fall: die, flowers, away	35
Faster than fairies, faster than witches	74
Foreign Lands	70
For I will consider my cat Jeoffry	20
Four seasons fill the measure	
of the year	30
From a Railway Carriage	74
From *Rain in Summer*	34
From *The Garden*	146
From *The Song of Solomon*	161
Full Fathom Five	56
Full fathom five they father lies	56
Gaily bedight	68
Glory be to God for dappled things	38
Good and Bad Children	84
He clasps the crag with crooked	
hands	23
Here a little child I stand	79
How beautiful is the rain!	34
How Doth the Little Crocodile	18
How doth the little crocodile	18
How do you like to go up in a swing	162
How Many Miles to Babylon?	92
How many miles to Babylon?	92
Hurt No Living Thing	16
Hurt no living thing	16
Hush Little Baby	93

Hush little baby, don't say a word   93

I Am of Ireland   152
I am of Ireland   152
I have a little shadow that goes in
    and out with me   40
I met a traveller from an antique land 66
In Sherwood lived stout Robin Hood 98
In the Highlands   158
In the highlands, in the country places 158
In winter I get up at night   88
In Xanadu did Kubla Khan   48
I Remember, I Remember   80
I remember, I remember   80
I Saw a Peacock   54
I saw a peacock with a fiery tail   54
I should like to rise and go   72
I Started Early   58
I started Early – Took my Dog   58
Is the Moon Tired?   89
Is the moon tired? She looks so pale   89
It was in and about the Martinmas
    time   112
It's Raining, It's Pouring   26
It's raining, it's pouring   26
I wandered lonely as a cloud   39

Jabberwocky   14
Jemima   123
John Barleycorn   134

Kubla Khan   48

La Belle Dame Sans Mercie   52
Listen to me, as when ye heard our
    father   156
Little Orphant Annie   76

Little Orphant Annie's come to our
    house to stay   76
Lochinvar   102

Margaret, are you grieving   155
Meeting at Night   64
Monday's Child   78
Monday's child is fair of face   78
Much have I travell'd in the realms
    of gold   143
Music   150
Music, when soft voices die   152
My beloved spake, and said unto me,
    Rise up, my love, my fair one, and
    come away   161
My Cat Jeoffry   20
My heart is like a singing bird   101
My love is like a red, red rose   100
My Shadow   40

Now's the time for mirth and play   161

O Captain! My Captain!   60
O Captain! my Captain! our fearful
    trip is done   60
"O whare are ye gaun?"   126
O, what can ail thee, knight-at-arms 52
O, young Lochinvar is come out of
    the west   102
*On First Looking into Chapman's
    Homer*   143
Once a jolly swagman camped by a
    billabong   132
Orpheus with his lute made trees   150
Ozymandias   66

Piano   151

Pied Beauty 38
Piping down the valleys wild 160
Piping Down the Valleys Wild 160

Requiem 163
Robin Hood 98

Shall I Compare thee to a
 Summer's Day? 45
Shall I compare thee to a
 summer's day 45
She Walks in Beauty 44
She walks in beauty, like the night 44
Sleep, Baby, Sleep! 94
Sleep, baby, sleep! 94
So, We'll Go No More A-Roving 154
So, we'll go no more a-roving 154
Softly, in the dusk, a woman is
 singing to me 151
Song's Eternity 148
Sound the Flute! 33
Spring 33
Spring and Fall 155
Star Light, Star Bright 92
Star light, star bright 92
Swing, Swing 82
Swing, swing 82
Symphony in Yellow 144

The Eagle 23
The Ecchoing Green 42
The Fairies 50
The False Knight and the Wee Boy 126
The Ghost's Song 133
The gray sea and the long black land 64
The Great Silkie of Sule Skerrie 114
The Herring Loves the Merry Moonlight 19

The herring loves the merry moonlight 19
The Human Seasons 30
The lights from the parlour and
 kitchen shone out 86
The Maldive Shark 19
The Night has a Thousand Eyes 106
The night has a thousand eyes 106
The North Wind Doth Blow 28
The north wind doth blow 28
The Owl 22
The Owl and the Pussy-cat 12
The Owl and the Pussy-Cat
 went to sea 12
The Oxen 140
The Rainbow 27
The Silver Swan 23
The silver swan, who living had
 no note 23
The splendour falls on castle walls 46
The sun does arise 42
The Swing 162
The Tyger 24
The Wind 28
The Yarn of the Nancy Bell 116
The Year's at the Spring 36
The year's at the spring 36
There was a little girl, and she wore
 a little curl 123
There Was a Naughty Boy 124
There was a naughty Boy 124
There was three Kings into the east 134
Thomas the Rhymer 108
To Emilia V— 152
To see a World in a Grain of Sand 16
Travel 72
True Thomas lay o'er yond grassy bank 108
'Twas brillig, and the slithy toves 14

'Twas on the shores that round our
    coast   116
Tyger! Tyger! burning bright   24

Under the wide and starry sky   163
Upon Westminster Bridge   142
Uphill   71
Up into the cherry-tree   70
Up the airy mountain   50

Wae's me! wae's me!   133
Waltzing Matilda   132
What Am I After All   122
What am I after all but a child, pleas'd
    with the sound of my own name?
    repeating it over and over   122
What Are Heavy?   57
What are heavy? sea-sand and sorrow   57
What is song's eternity?   148
What wondorous life in this I lead!   146
When cats run home and light is come   22
When in Disgrace with Fortune   159

When in disgrace with fortune and
    men's eyes   159
*When That I was and a Little
    Tiny Boy*   130
When that I was and a little
    tiny boy   130
Whenever the moon and stars are set   29
When icicles hang by the wall   32
Where Lies the Land   67
Where lies the land to which the
    ship would go?   67
Whether the Weather Be Fine   26
Whether the weather be fine   26
Who has seen the wind?   28
Windy nights   29
Winter   32
Wynken, Blynken, and Nod   90
Wynken, Blynken, and Nod
    one night   90